THE BURNING OF CORK

*This book is dedicated
to
the people of Cork
past, present and future*

THE BURNING
OF CORK

GERRY WHITE
&
BRENDAN O'SHEA

MERCIER PRESS
WHAT YOU NEED TO READ

Mercier Press
Douglas Village, Cork
www.mercierpress.ie

Trade enquiries to Columba Mercier Distribution,
55a Spruce Avenue, Stillorgan Industrial Park, Blackrock, Dublin

ISBN: 1 85635 522 5 / 978 1 85635 522 3

10 9 8 7 6 5 4 3 2 1

Mercier Press receives financial assistance from
the Arts Council/An Chomhairle Ealaíon

Printed and Bound by J. H. Haynes & Co. Ltd, Sparkford

CONTENTS

ACKNOWLEDGEMENTS

This book had its origins in the summer of 2005, when John Dolan, the features editor with the *Evening Echo* asked us to write an article about the burning of Cork on the night of 11/12 December 1920 for that year's *Holly Bough*. Coincidently, while we were working on this article, we were approached by Cónal Creedon who asked us to take part in a documentary on the burning of the city which he was then preparing for RTÉ. In that respect both John and Cónal were in at the birth of this book and we are grateful to both of them for their encouragement.

Numerous people provided us with invaluable assistance without which this book would not have been finished. Accordingly we must acknowledge Comdt Victor Laing, Sgt Chris Donovan and Pte Alan Manning of the Military Archives, Cathal Brugha Barracks, Dublin for accessing material from the Bureau of Military History; John Borgonovo for providing us with a copy of his MA thesis, *Informers, Intelligence and the 'Anti-Sinn Fein Society' – the Anglo-Irish Conflict in Cork City 1920–1921* and for sharing his expertise on this particular subject with us on many occasions; Kevin Girvan for providing us with a copy of his M Phil thesis, *The Life and Times of Seán O'Hegarty;* Tom and Dick O'Mahony for providing us with information about the Dillon's Cross ambush as related to them over the years by their father, Volunteer James O'Mahony; Stephen Leach, Lucy Stewart, Caroline Long-Nolan and Jamie O'Connell at the Local Studies Department in Cork City Library; Stella Cherry and Dan Breen at Cork Public Museum; Brian McGee and the staff of the Cork Archives Institute; Jim Herlihy for sharing his knowledge of the RIC and the Auxiliary Division; Pat Poland for sharing his knowledge of the Cork Fire

Brigade; Des Garrett for supplying us with biographical details of Alfred Hutson; Antón O'Callaghan at RTÉ Cork: Íde Aherne and Marion Geoghegan at the Radio Archives Project in Limerick; Malachy Moran at RTÉ Radio Dublin; Anne Kearney at the *Irish Examiner;* Pat Cremin at the Collins Barracks Military Museum; Susan Durack at the library at NUI Maynooth; Tom O'Neill, Gerard Murphy, Tommy Goodchild and Bertie Bowman for sharing their knowledge at critical times; Fr Donal O'Donovan and Pat McCarthy of the Dunmanway Historical Society for helping us with our research into the deaths of Canon Magner and Tadgh Crowley; Peter Berresford Ellis for providing the invaluable report into the burning of Cork written by his late father Alan Ellis; Colin Ó Laochdha for willingly providing his excellent painting of City Hall in flames for the cover; Marie O'Brien for typing several documents; and Jim Scanlon, Tim Long, Karen O'Neill, Brian Coniry, Dave Heaphy, Seán Dunne, Eugene Power and Tim Egar for their personal support throughout.

However one person deserves special mention, both for his own personal dedication to the preservation of the history of his native city, and for unconditionally providing us with an endless supply for documentation and analysis. That person is Dick Kenny, son of Lt Michael Kenny Cork No. 1 Brigade, Irish Volunteers.

Finally, and as always, we are extremely grateful for the unswerving support of the White and O'Shea families without which this book, or indeed any of our other work, would not have been possible. They have long since forgotten the funny side of our historical pursuits and have been faced instead with lengthy periods of absence, innumerable sullen moods, and the inability to acquire time on the telephone for even local calls. Suffice to say the word 'thanks' can never be enough.

Gerry White & Brendan O'Shea
Cork City
12 September 2006

FOREWORD

On 11 December 1920, Cork city was to experience an unimaginable night of terror and destruction. Large tracts of the city were destroyed by fire including the residential area of Dillon's Cross and the commercial heart of the city centre. South of the river, incendiaries also levelled the administrative centre at City Hall and the Carnegie Library. Business premises were looted, citizens were intimidated and firemen were shot and wounded as they fought the flames. Then, as if a bookend to that night's carnage, a death squad made its way to the Delany home on Dublin Hill, where two brothers Con and Jerh Delany were shot dead and their uncle William Dunlea was wounded.

Some time ago, I came across a handful of photographs depicting the scenes of devastation in the aftermath of that night. There was a bleak eeriness about those images of December 1920. It was the week leading into Christmas, citizens gathered looking on helplessly as their city centre lay in smouldering ruins. I trawled over the photos in the hope of finding some familiar landmark, eventually identifying the gable end of the Lee Cinema on Winthrop Street still standing testament to the horrors of that night.

My curiosity was to develop into a more in-depth research. It struck me as extraordinary that an event of such magnitude could have occurred within living memory – and yet leave little or no imprint on the collective consciousness of the people of Cork. Even the streetscape of the city seemed to have risen Phoenix-like and bears no trace, nor tell-tale scars.

Eventually, a window into Cork's past opened up for me. It was a small city, a city that traded comfortably as a hub of the commercial network of the empire. A city that welcomed royal visits, and whose menfolk for generations had a proud tradition of enlisting to fight for monarch and country.

But it was also a city with a strong nationalist heritage, represented in the House of Commons for over a decade by Charles Stewart Parnell, the uncrowned king of Ireland. It was a city where the Molly Maguires and the All For Irelanders clashed publicly on conflicting views of nationalism, a city where IRB secrecy remained intact.

This complex political landscape was typified by the fact that while the Cork Brigade of the Irish Volunteers mobilised for the 1916 Rising to break the link with Britain, many thousands of fellow Corkmen had joined the Irish regiments of the British army to fight in First World War for the freedom of small nations.

Gradually, in the course of my research, names such as Mac-Swiney, MacCurtain, Walsh, Delany, de Róiste, Fawsitt, Lynch, Langford, Murtagh, Strickland, Smyth and many, many more began to take the form of real flesh-and-blood people, people who walked the streets of my city. People whose actions ultimately inspired me to make *The Burning of Cork*, a television documentary on the subject.

I'm not a historian, I'm an enthusiast and maybe that explains why sometimes I have felt like a water beetle just skimming the surface of a very deep well. The work has taken me on a journey I could never have anticipated. And the highlight for me must be the people I have met along the way – far too many to mention by name here.

The moment I first saw those old photographs of the smoking ruins of Cork city, it was inevitable that I would cross paths with Brendan O'Shea and Gerry White. I had been aware of their various published works and research into the Irish Volunteers. And at that time, they had completed preliminary research on the events surrounding the burning of Cork for a series of articles that were subsequently published in 2005. They were in the process of laying down the foundations for this book.

So I was delighted when they agreed without hesitation to talk to me about participating in the documentary.

That first meeting was highly charged as we shared anecdotes and compared gems we'd uncovered in our respective research. It was to be the first of many such meetings: sometimes social, sometimes focused on work in progress, but always highly engaging and enlightening.

In researching and presenting history, Gerry and Brendan have developed a highly effective working relationship. Anyone who has witnessed their public lectures will immediately recognise the dynamic and complementary nature of their collaboration.

But the same is true for their published work – where again the attention to fact and detail is counterbalanced by well-formed insightful observation.

In this volume Brendan O'Shea and Gerry White meticulously recount and contextualise the events surrounding the burning of Cork. It is a journey sure to reawaken subliminal memories buried deep in the consciousness of Cork City. It is a journey well worth taking ...

CÓNAL CREEDON
DIRECTOR,
THE BURNING OF CORK
RTÉ HIDDEN HISTORIES SERIES

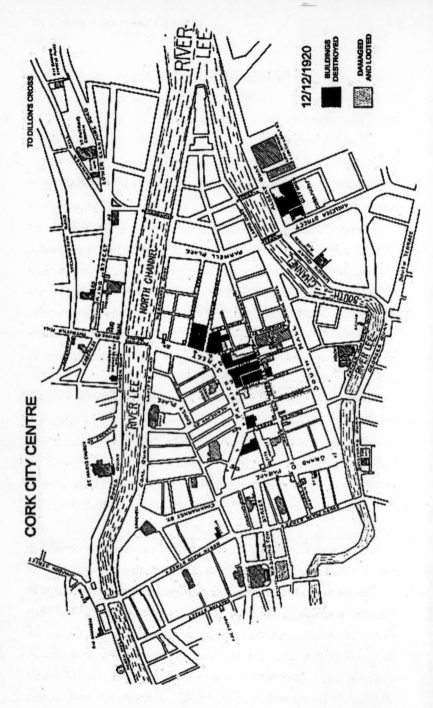

Map depicting damage to Cork City centre from *Who Burnt Cork City?*
(Irish Labour and Trade Union Congress, Dublin, 1921)

INTRODUCTION

It was bitterly cold that Saturday morning, 11 December 1920, as the citizens of Cork made their way into town with varying degrees of urgency. Those who had sufficient money in their pockets could be seen walking down St Patrick's Street visiting Roche's Stores, Cash's, the Munster Arcade, Egan's Jewellers and the Saxone Shoe Shop to start their Christmas shopping. Others with lesser means made their purchases on the Coal Quay and then sought out the relative comfort of the English Market where, protected from the elements, they could marvel at the meat and vegetable stalls in anticipation of some small treat two weeks hence.

For the more educated, there was the prospect of a quiet hour or two in the solitude of the Carnegie Free Library on Anglesea Street, while the affluent could wander down to Emmet Place and book their seats for the last performance of *The Gondoliers* which was playing at the Opera House that night. And at several locations along the streets, the paper boys were selling the *Holly Bough*.

Yes, it was Christmas time in Cork, but this was deceptive because that morning Ireland was also a country at war.

The previous nine months had witnessed a significant upsurge in violence as attacks by the Irish Volunteers on crown forces had been met in turn by the imposition of curfew during hours of darkness and savage un-official reprisals in the form of shootings and arson attacks. Cork city and county were now at boiling point with the Volunteers and those who opposed them operating in a very murky world where one man's freedom fighter was the other's terrorist. The established forces of law and order were slowly but surely losing the initiative and counter-insurgency tactics were no longer working against a guerrilla army whose soldiers could envelop themselves in a cloak of invisibility after each attack by disappearing back into the civilian population where they were free to plot the next violent encounter.

Each morning, the duty officers in Victoria Barracks and at the RIC headquarters on Union Quay reported to their superiors on growing casualty lists, continuing violent attacks, and increased incident and tension levels. Political pressure from London now increased on a daily basis. Martial Law had been imposed, but the military and police commanders on the ground were still unable to fight the enemy for the simple reason that they could not see him.

If this pattern continued – and there was every reason to expect it would – then those who harboured the enemy were certain to become the focus of military operations. By now that group comprised the majority of the nationalist population which made the strategy employed by the Volunteers very high risk.

As the military and police operations staffs in Victoria Barracks and at Union Quay grappled with increasing violence and the corresponding failure of the reprisals carried out to date, the only question of consequence was how long more this war of attrition would continue? How many more lives were going to be lost? Could the practice of violent reprisal, which often included razing homes and business premises to the ground, continue to be tolerated?

Little did anybody realise that morning as they went about their business that before a new day dawned another ambush would be launched and a major reprisal on a scale hitherto unseen in the conflict would take place – and the physical geography of the centre of Cork city would be transformed forever.

1

REORGANISATION

Disillusioned with the strategy of open warfare which had failed so spectacularly in 1916, the leaders of the Irish Volunteers who survived the Easter Rising soon began laying the groundwork for the next phase of Ireland's fight for freedom. Once released from prison their first task was to rebuild the Volunteer movement into a credible military force. In Cork, this responsibility fell to Tomás MacCurtain, the officer commanding the Cork Brigade, who was released from Frongoch Camp in Wales at Christmas 1916.[1]

MacCurtain, assisted by Terence MacSwiney and Seán O'Hegarty, and a completely new generation of Volunteers like Florence O'Donoghue, quickly had the brigade back on its feet, and although many of the leaders were re-arrested in 1917, the unit managed to resume several activities.[2] On 12 July 1917, they paraded through the city to celebrate de Valera's victory in the Clare by-election, and on 5 September, a number of Volunteers raided the Cork Grammar School on Wellington Road and removed a quantity of weapons stored there for use by the school's Officer Training Corps. Then on 27 September, in another very public demonstration, they paraded in Dublin at the funeral of Thomas Ashe, just as they had at O'Donovan Rossa's funeral two years previously.

Meanwhile, the First World War continued, with the British army sustaining huge casualties on the Western Front. Faced with the unthinkable prospect of defeat in the trenches, on 16 April 1918, the House of Commons passed the Military Conscription

Bill, extending compulsory military service to Ireland. This decision generated widespread anger amongst all shades of Irish nationalism and had the effect of temporarily uniting Irish nationalist MPs at Westminster, Sinn Féin, the Irish Volunteers, and the Catholic Church in determined opposition with over two million people signing an anti-conscription pledge on 21 April.

With the British now facing an acute shortage of military manpower, and the Volunteer movement clearly regenerating in Ireland, the colonial secretary, Walter Long, and the new viceroy, Lord French, held several meetings in London between 6–10 May 1918 and it was decided to once again adopt a hard-line Irish policy.[3] The results were immediate. On the morning of 17 May 1918, a major security operation got underway in Dublin during which over eighty senior republican figures were arrested. Those who evaded capture went 'on the run' and were forced into a clandestine life. Michael Collins, the Volunteer's Director of Organisation, focused on rebuilding the movement and setting up an intelligence network, while Chief of Staff, Richard Mulcahy, concentrated on restraining the more radical Volunteers from embarking on an open military conflict which they could not possibly win.

In the anti-conscription campaign which followed the Cork Brigade played a very active and public role, but in spite of Mulcahy's reservations a decision was taken at local level by militant volunteers to step up military activity. One such operation was mounted on 12 September 1918 when a party of soldiers was successfully relieved of their weapons at the bottom of Richmond Hill. Responding to this activity the RIC moved against a number of Volunteer activists and on 4 November, Captain Donnacha MacNeilus was arrested at his lodgings in Leitrim Street. In the scuffle which ensued, MacNeilus grabbed a revolver and shot and seriously wounded Head Constable Clarke. Police reinforcements, led by District Inspector Oswald Swanzy, overcame MacNeilus and he was arrested and taken prisoner to Cork Gaol. With the threat of execution hanging over MacNeilus if Head Constable Clarke died from his wounds, on 11 November a party of Volunteers managed to enter the gaol, overcome the guards, and rescue MacNeilus.

Ironically, that same day, the First World War ended but the impact of that event was not destined to restore stability in Ireland. In fact it had the opposite effect and, when a general election was held on 14 December, it returned Sinn Féin with seventy-three seats, the Unionists with twenty-six seats, and the Irish Party decimated returning a mere six MPs. The result was a massive victory for Sinn Féin but it also greatly enhanced the moral authority of the Volunteers and effectively left both organisations with a popular mandate to continue their efforts in pursuit of an Irish Republic.

The wave of nationalism that swept Ireland in the aftermath of the Easter Rebellion, combined with the subsequent threat of conscription, had resulted in thousands of young men joining the ranks of the Volunteers. By Christmas 1918, the strength of the Cork Brigade stood at just over 8,000 men. These were sub-divided into twenty battalions with eight companies in each, although the actual strength of these formations varied from parish to parish.

Volunteer headquarters in Dublin now decided to reorganise a number of the larger units to cope with the expanding numbers. In January 1919, the Cork Brigade was reconfigured to consist of the Cork No. 1 Brigade (Cork city and mid Cork, commanded by Tomás MacCurtain), Cork No. 2 Brigade (north Cork, commanded by Liam Lynch), and Cork No. 3 Brigade (west Cork, commanded by Tom Hales).[4] The headquarters of Cork No. 1 Brigade was located at the home of the Wallace sisters, Nora and Shelia, at 86 Brunswick Street (now St Augustine's Street) in Cork city. No. 1 Battalion was situated north of the River Lee, No. 2 Battalion was located south of the river, the remaining eight battalions were located in surrounding towns, and, to cater for the spiritual needs of the Volunteers, Fr Dominic O'Connor, OFM, was appointed the brigade chaplain.[5]

Then, on 21 January 1919, the struggle for independence entered a new phase when twenty-eight Sinn Féin members of the Westminster parliament, who had been elected at the general election on 14 December, gathered at the Mansion House in Dublin and established Dáil Éireann as the independent constituent assembly of the Irish nation.[6] They ratified both a declaration of independence, which established an independent Irish Republic, and a democratic programme, which enshrined the principles by which the new republic would be governed.

However, not all Volunteers welcomed the development. Some within the movement continued to believe that constitutional means alone would never produce an Irish Republic and so, lest numbers begin to fall, and the Volunteer organisation become complacent, a number of the more militant republicans decided to take matters into their own hands.

On the very day the Dáil was established, Volunteers from the Tipperary No. 3 Brigade, led by Dan Breen and Seán Treacy, mounted an attack on a party of RIC who were escorting a cartload of explosives to the Soloheadbeg quarry. Two RIC constables, James McDonnell and Patrick O'Connell, were killed and the Volunteers made off with their weapons and the explosives. While a number of minor attacks against members of the RIC had taken place before Soloheadbeg, this incident was hugely significant. In fact it turned out to be the beginning of what would become the War of Independence. Ten days later, the Irish Volunteers' journal, *An tÓglach*, declared that the Volunteers were 'entitled morally and legally to kill British police and soldiers'.

Within weeks Volunteer units across the country were carrying out similar operations. As attacks on the RIC increased, the British government responded by proclaiming on 10 April that the following areas were in 'a state of disturbance': Cork City, Cork East and Cork West Ridings, County Kerry, County Limerick and City, County Roscommon and Tipperary North and South Ridings.[7] By May 1919, Lord French was becoming so frustrated with the security situation that he complained to his staff: 'every day brings fresh proof of the underground actions of these Irish Volunteers which are nothing more or less than a regular constituted and organised Sinn Féin army'.[8]

On 20 August 1919, the Dáil, took another significant step towards establishing democracy when a motion proposed by the minister for defence, Cathal Brugha, was passed making it compulsory for all members of the Volunteers to swear an oath of allegiance to the Dáil. This effectively brought the Volunteers under Dáil control and made them the *de facto* army of the Irish Republic. From this time onwards the terms Irish Volunteers, *Óglaigh na hÉireann*, and Irish Republican Army became inter-changeable. In most respects, this development was purely cosmetic because on the ground nothing changed at all, especially in Cork where the Volunteers were still opposed by the vastly superior forces of the British army and the RIC.

The most potent symbol of British rule in Cork city at that time was the sprawling military complex at Victoria Barracks. It housed the headquarters of the 6th Infantry Division commanded by General Sir E. P. Strickland, KCB, KBE, CMG, DSO, whose designated area of operations encompassed the entire province of Munster.[9] The barracks also contained the headquarters of the 17th Infantry Brigade commanded by Brigadier General Harold Whitla Higginson, DSO, and two infantry battalions from this unit formed the permanent garrison which had responsibility for operations in Cork city.[10]

Responsibility for policing within the city and county, fell to the Royal Irish Constabularly (RIC) which at that time was also a formidable and credible force. Formed as the 'Irish Constabulary' in 1836 this armed police force had earned the prefix 'royal' for its role in the suppression of the Fenian Rising of 1867. Members wore a dark green uniform and were recruited from every parish in the country. With the exception of the capital city, which was policed by the Dublin Metropolitan Police, the RIC had barracks located in every town and city in the country. In Cork city, their headquarters was located at Union Quay Barracks, with other stations at the Bridewell, Blackrock, Barrack Street, Commons Road, Douglas, King Street, North Abbey Street, St Luke's, South Infirmary Road, Sunday's Well, Watercourse Road, Togher and Tuckey Street.

Throughout 1919, although some Volunteers conducted a number of low level operations, it was also clear that a wave of frustration was building with Mulcahy's policy of military inaction. In tandem with this, or perhaps because of it, a rift began to emerge between those Volunteers answering exclusively to GHQ and those Volunteers still members of the IRB and operating within two parallel chains of command. In Cork, this manifested itself in difficulties between MacCurtain, who had resigned from the IRB at Christmas 1916, and his vice commandant, Seán O'Hegarty, who was also head of the IRB in the city.

The issue came to a head one night at the end of April 1919 when Volunteer Harry Varian was making his way home and Constable John Hayes attempted to stop and question him. Varian, who had consumed several drinks, pulled a gun and fired it, seriously wounding the policeman. The following day the homes of known Volunteers were raided and many were arrested and questioned about the attack. Fred Murray, who bore some resemblance to Varian, and whom the wounded policeman mistakenly identified as his assailant, was arrested and charged on 15 May. He was remanded for trial before a special jury at the summer assizes on 28 July.[11]

From MacCurtain's perspective, this was a complete mess. He knew Murray was not involved but he had no idea who had actually fired the shots. It then transpired that Varian had told his IRB superior, Seán O'Hegarty, of his role in the incident and that O'Hegarty had decided not to mention it to MacCurtain because he deemed it exclusively an IRB matter. When Florrie O'Donoghue discovered this he told MacCurtain the truth and Varian was formally paraded in front of the Volunteer brigade staff and questioned. Far from repentant, he declared that he had Seán O'Hegarty's authority to carry a gun and use it if need be.

MacCurtain was outraged both by Varian's attitude and the fact that the whole matter was in effect a direct challenge to his authority as the brigade commander. The incident also brought to a head the issue of command and control within the brigade as a whole and specifically the matter of who controlled the weapons supplied to the Volunteers by the IRB organisation. At Easter 1916 the issue of parallel chains of command had been at the core of the brigade commander's difficulties and three years later it clearly remained unresolved.

MacCurtain had discontinued his own IRB membership after 1916 for this very reason. He firmly believed there was no longer any need for such a secret organisation and this view was shared by Éamon de Valera, Cathal Brugha and several others. They advocated that the fight for independence be undertaken by political and military organisations that were open and visible to the Irish people. Parallel chains of command had failed abysmally in 1916 and from MacCurtain's perspective could only lead to failure once again. He saw the Varian case as ample proof of this, if further proof were needed.

However, other officers including Michael Collins, O'Donoghue and O'Hegarty, believed that the IRB still had a role to play and O'Donoghue summed up the position from his perspective:

> knowing the composition of the Volunteer mentality at the time, knowing the absence of official policy, and believing that whatever was attempted would emanate from the driving force of I.R.B. men within its ranks, I had become convinced of the necessity of maintaining the organisation notwithstanding all the difficulties and dangers of dual control.[12]

In any event, now that MacCurtain was finally in possession of all the facts he was also faced with a dilemma. He did not want to divide the brigade which he had helped found and then re-organised with such great effort. Nevertheless, he could not countenance the existence of parallel chains of command within his own unit. For his part, O'Hegarty refused to relinquish any of his authority as leader of the IRB in Cork but said that he was still more than willing to continue serving in the Volunteers under MacCurtain's command.

O'Donoghue, who was close to both officers and considered them to be his friends as well as his comrades, fully accepted that each was acting out of a strong sense of duty and that the situation wasn't complicated by bitterness or ambition. A compromise would have to be reached and eventually it was. O'Hegarty would resign as vice commandant of the brigade and return to the ranks as an ordinary Volunteer. This would leave MacCurtain's authority as brigade commander secure and O'Hegarty's IRB position intact. It also left the way open for Terence MacSwiney to be appointed brigade vice commandant.

But in many ways these were the least of MacCurtain's problems. He was also faced with the growing challenge of keeping his brigade united in the face of clear instructions from GHQ in Dublin not to engage in major military action – and this was proving exceptionally difficult.

There was disaffection within MacCurtain's command where the more militant Volunteers were clamouring for action. The challenge now facing MacCurtain was to plan and execute realistic, achievable and meaningful military action which would facilitate and maintain unity of command. He still bore the mental scars from having failed to order rebellion at Easter 1916 and understood that engaging in pitched battles against a far superior enemy was no way to win a war. It had to be done some other way, but, most importantly, it had to be approved by GHQ.

Also frustrated with inaction was Cork No. 2 Brigade under the command of Liam Lynch and, on 7 September, twenty-five Volunteers with six revolvers between them took matters into their own hands. Dressed in civilian attire they ambushed a detachment from the King's Shropshire Light Infantry on their way to the Wesleyan church in Fermoy. One soldier was killed, three were wounded, and fifteen rifles were captured in what was the first action against military forces since the Easter Rising. The following night soldiers from the nearby barracks descended on Fermoy smashing the windows of several shops and looting large quantities of goods. Tensions remained high until Thursday by which time several known Volunteers had been arrested and the town returned to relative normality.

Responding to this attack, and taking account of the ripple of violence and discontent now sweeping the country, King George V immediately sought some response from the government. Under pressure to take some action, Prime Minister Lloyd George and Chief Secretary Bonar Law finally decided to act and, on the morning of 12 September, the Dáil was suppressed by vice-regal proclamation. This was a critical moment. Up to that point the Volunteer chief-of-staff, Richard Mulcahy, had been actively trying to curtail Volunteer operations in the country – he now decided the time had come to turn them loose.[13]

This was the opportunity MacCurtain had been waiting for and he produced an offensive plan to attack a number of RIC barracks based on a very simple strategy. The weakest link in the security framework was unquestionably the RIC. They lived and worked for the most part within small rural communities where they were the 'eyes and ears' of the British administration in Ireland. The removal of these officers would curtail or eliminate the flow of local intelligence which was finding its way to Dublin Castle. If the RIC could also be intimidated into actually abandoning their barracks and leaving these towns and villages altogether, then so much the better. Vast swathes of the countryside would then have no police presence and allow the Volunteers complete freedom to operate as they pleased. These same RIC barracks would also provide a ready source of arms and ammunition of which the Volunteers were in dire need and it was with this plan that MacCurtain and MacSwiney approached GHQ in mid-November 1919. Meeting at Cullenswood House in Ranelagh, Mulcahy approved MacCurtain's plan but stipulated that 'every man involved must be at his work the next day as if no dog had barked in the place.'[14] So on 2 January 1920, Cork No. 1 Brigade launched simultaneous attacks on the RIC barracks at Kilmurray and Carrigtwohill in what were effectively the first 'official' Volunteer attacks of the Anglo-Irish war.

While the RIC garrison at Kilmurray managed to mount a successful defence and repel the attackers, the operation at Carrigtwohill had a very different outcome. That night a party of Volunteers drawn from the Cobh and Midleton companies of the 4th Battalion under the command of Commandant Michael Leahy made their way into the village. Leahy later recalled:

About 11 p.m. when I had satisfied myself that every man was in his allotted position, I gave orders to open the attack. Fire was begun by our riflemen in front and from those in the rear. Grenades were flung at the barrack windows, but, because of the steel shutters on the windows, did no damage. The R.I.C. replied with rifle fire and grenades. Verey lights were sent up by the garrison. This continued for about quarter of an hour when I concluded that our fire was ineffective and had no chance of forcing a surrender on the R.I.C., I, therefore, ordered that the gable end of the barrack wall be dynamited with a view to obtaining entrance and taking the place by assault.

John Moore, from Cobh, was deputed for the job. A few men bored about five holes in the barrack wall while John inserted the sticks of gelignite. Constant fire was kept up on the R.I.C. to cover the men engaged in this operation. About an hour elapsed before this was completed; meanwhile the garrison in the barracks kept up a continuous fire with rifles and grenades. Our men replied sporadically.

When the dynamite exploded, a large hole was blown in the gable end of the barracks sufficient to admit two men at a time into what was the barrack dayroom. Bundles of hay soaked with petrol were placed in the breach. It was my intention to 'burn out' the garrison. At the last minute I decided against doing so as I learned that three of our lads had been taken prisoner earlier in the night and were now in the barracks. I, therefore, decided to enter the barracks by the breach in the wall and call upon the garrison to surrender.

About four of us, including Joseph Aherne and Diarmuid Hurley, got through the hole into the dayroom and found that the R.I.C. had taken to the rooms upstairs. We fired a few shots through the ceiling. Before entering I had sent word to all my men in firing positions to cease firing at a whistle blast given by me. I blew the whistle when we were in the dayroom; our lads ceased fire and I shouted to the police that we were inside the barracks and that they should surrender. At the top of the stairs I saw Mrs. Casey, wife of the R.I.C. sergeant, with a baby in her arms. The sergeant was behind her. I told the woman to come on down, that nothing would happen to her and ordered the sergeant to stay where he was and keep his hands up. He did this. Mrs. Casey and her baby were then taken by one of our lads to friends of hers in the village.

I again called on the garrison to surrender. They did so, coming downstairs with their hands up.[15]

Leahy then handcuffed all the RIC officers together and locked them into the building before driving off with their arms and ammunition in a car he had commandeered earlier that morning. The capture of Carrigtwohill RIC barracks was the first successful Volunteer operation of its kind and proved just how vulnerable these isolated garrisons actually were. It was also a clear indication of how the emerging conflict would be fought.

2

THE DEATH OF MACCURTAIN

After Carrigtwohill, Volunteer attacks on the RIC became more frequent. In response, many constables opted to resign from the force – some out of fear for their lives and the lives of their families, others for more patriotic reasons. As their strength decreased, manning the more isolated barracks became untenable. When these constables were re-deployed into the towns and cities most of the deserted barracks were burned to the ground. Where once the RIC had been a highly respected institution within the community, now many of these officers and their families were pariahs; shopkeepers refused to supply them and former friends and neighbours either openly ostracised them or simply stayed away. It had long been a source of pride in families to have a son progressing through the ranks of the RIC but now this was becoming a serious liability. Slowly but surely the will of many to continue in service was being eroded.

For those officers who chose to remain within its ranks, it was inevitable that they would attempt to carry out their orders with a steely purpose and determination. The Volunteers might well be fighting for a republic but the RIC were fighting now to preserve their own way of life. Both sides were actually fighting for survival – it was in fact a civil war where the stakes could not have been higher.

In an attempt to maintain the strength of the RIC and regain some control of the countryside, the British government now decided to begin advertising in Britain to attract new recruits into the force. The campaign began at the end of January 1920 and, with wages advertised at ten shillings per day all found, hundreds of unemployed ex-servicemen were quick to come forward. It would be some time before this initiative had an impact in Cork, where in tandem with the revolutionary campaign, a political upheaval was also underway.

Having returned two Sinn Féin candidates, J. J. Walsh and Liam de Róiste, at the 1918 general election, the municipal elections of January 1920 presented the citizens of Cork with another opportunity to indicate their approval for the struggle for independence. When the ballots were counted the results were unambiguous: of the fifty-six members elected to the Corporation thirty were members of Sinn Féin and, when the new council held its first meeting in City Hall on the night of Friday, 30 January 1920, Tomás MacCurtain was elected lord mayor. In a clear statement of future intent, MacCurtain's first official act was to propose, and have passed, a resolution in which the corporation recognised the suppressed Dáil Éireann as the legal and lawfully constituted parliament of Ireland and the executive of the Dáil as the lawful government.

This was a singularly courageous move, especially since it was public knowledge that MacCurtain still retained his position as commanding officer of Cork No. 1 Brigade of the Volunteers and so bore full responsibility for the military campaign being waged against the crown. However, it is far from clear whether MacCurtain had complete control over all members of his unit at this time. By presenting himself for election, becoming lord mayor, resigning from the IRB, and adhering rigidly to the Volunteer chain of command, it was inevitable that he would distance himself somewhat from O'Hegarty and the more militant Volunteers within the brigade.

In parallel to developments at City Hall, both the Volunteers and the crown forces in Cork city now became involved in an 'Intelligence War'. The RIC and the military depended on information supplied by loyal citizens and paid informers, and while both organisations had their own intelligence staffs, they also co-ordinated their efforts and produced agreed intelligence summaries. The man responsible for synchronising this work was Captain James Kelly, the intelligence officer on the staff of the Sixth Division headquarters at Victoria Barracks – and his work proved to be very effective.

Within the Volunteer organisation, Kelly's opposite number was Captain Florrie O'Donoghue, Cork No. 1 Brigade's intelligence officer who was at ease living and working in the murky world of espionage and counter-intelligence. O'Donoghue quickly established a basic organisation in every company and battalion area as well as a wide network of sources in the Post Office and Telephone Exchange. He also identified how the civilian population could be utilised and divided them into three categories:

> First, those who would help us as far as they could, and they were the majority, second, those who would stand aloof either through indifference or fear, and third, the minority who would help our enemies. For the acquisition of information we organised a wide variety of contacts designed to make the maximum use of those who would help, particularly where they were favourably placed for the purpose.

In relation to counter-intelligence he believed that:

> the minority who would aid the enemy could be divided into two distinct classes – the members of England's faithful garrison of civilians, and the mercenary touts and pimps, usually local and native. The first were by far the more potentially dangerous.

They were not merely hostile, they were anti-Irish and regarded themselves as honoured in any service they could do for England. They were in the main intelligent observers, they had wide business and social contacts and the Masonic cement kept them well integrated. The second class, contemptible and unprincipled, were men of such limited range and ability that their value to the enemy must have been slight.[16]

Late in 1919 O'Donoghue was tasked by brigade headquarters with establishing a full-time brigade intelligence squad and the men selected were Jeremiah O'Brien, Jim Fitzgerald, Denis Hegarty, Frank Mahony, Bob Aherne and Michael Kenny. O'Donoghue later recalled that:

The work which these men were called upon to do was extremely dangerous and in the conditions prevailing in the city at the time, could only be performed by men of exceptional courage and resource. The fact that the Intelligence Department of Cork No. 1 Brigade was congratulated on several occasions by the Director of Intelligence is the best proof of the efficient manner in which they carried out their onerous duties.[17]

Accordingly, by 1920 O'Donoghue was running an extensive network of agents consisting of republican sympathisers working in hotels, civic clubs, pubs, post offices and railway stations throughout the city. Utilising all these assets he scored a significant success in February 1920 when Timothy Quinlisk, a former member of Roger Casement's Irish Brigade, was unmasked as a spy and executed.[18] He was also able to provide reliable information to assist in the planning of operations and, on 10 March, he participated in an attack on RIC District Inspector McDonagh and Sergeant Ferris in which the former was wounded.

In response, the RIC raided and ransacked two Sinn Féin halls and the homes of a number of prominent republicans. Daniel Cohalan, the Roman Catholic Bishop of Cork, denounced the Volunteers' action from the pulpit of the North Cathedral declaring that a campaign against the police was a campaign against public order. But, undeterred by the bishop's warning, at 11 p.m. on the night of 19 March, another attack was mounted and RIC Constable Joseph Murtagh was shot dead as he walked along Pope's Quay. He was returning to his home on Sunday's Well Road having attended the funeral of an RIC constable who had been killed two days earlier. According to Volunteer Patrick 'Pa' Murray, Murtagh was shot by two men under his command, Christy MacSwiney and J. J. O'Connell, 'on orders from brigade'.[19] Murtagh was considered to have used extreme methods while trying to extract information from Martin Condon, a Volunteer from Cork No. 2 Brigade, who was, at that time, in custody in the Military Detention Barracks.

The killing of Constable Murtagh was quickly followed by an incident which even O'Donoghue could not have foreseen, the reverberations from which were destined to be felt throughout Cork city and county, and indeed, in the country as a whole. At approximately 1 a.m. on the morning of Saturday, 20 March, armed men with blackened faces surrounded the home of Tomás MacCurtain at 40 Thomas Davis Street, Blackpool. They banged incessantly on the door until his wife, Eilís, eventually opened it. She was held to one side as two men charged upstairs where they shot and killed her husband as he was coming out of his bedroom.

At around 3 a.m. Florrie O'Donoghue was awakened at his home at 55 North Main Street by Volunteer Michael Barrett and told that his commanding officer had just been shot dead by the police. Shocked and stunned by the news he pulled on his clothes and rushed over to MacCurtain's home where he had to push his way through the crowds gathering outside. Making his way upstairs he found the body of his commanding officer lying in his bed. 'I looked into his quiet dead face,' he later recalled, 'all the bullets had been fired at his body and except for a wound on one finger he was not visibly disfigured. His poor wife was in a state of collapse; the house was filled with the wailing of his young children, and Father Dominic who had arrived just ahead of me was doing his best to console them.'[20] It was the morning of MacCurtain's thirty-sixth birthday.

This was a tragedy of huge proportions. Tomas MacCurtain was the lord mayor of Cork – the first republican to hold that office. He offered real hope for the future to the nationalist population of the city. But he was also the brigade commander of the Cork No. 1 Brigade and, since 1916, had supervised the resurgence of the Volunteer movement in the city and county.

As brigade commander MacCurtain answered to Mulcahy for everything his brigade did and failed to do, but within the brigade some Volunteers who were also members of the IRB were now undertaking operations on their own. In this regard there is no direct evidence to indicate that MacCurtain either planned or approved the attacks on McDonagh, Ferris or Murtagh, and while Pa Murray did state that Murtagh had been shot 'on orders from brigade' he never claimed that MacCurtain had personally ordered the attack. In fact it is well established that MacCurtain actually contacted the hospital enquiring after Murtagh's health, an act which was singularly out of character for a Volunteer commander who might, some hours previously, have ordered the constable's execution.[21] Additionally, there is evidence which indicates that MacCurtain intended to have Murtagh's assailants called to account for their actions and Volunteer Cornelius Kelliher later stated that he was aware that MacCurtain was going to make Murtagh's killers 'pay the piper for shooting police on their own'.

22

In tandem with his military role, MacCurtain was also a very hard-working lord mayor, but it is clear that some elements within the British security forces considered him nothing more than a terrorist who played politics by day and revolution by night. As far as these people were concerned, the Volunteers who carried out every attack on the RIC within the city were under MacCurtain's command – and working with his approval. Within the police and military a perception prevailed that MacCurtain was the one who bore full responsibility for these attacks and, given that he never publicly denounced them, he had, in that sense, and in the context of the time, made himself a prime target for a reprisal killing.

Michael J. Feeley, a former senior sergeant in the RIC, later confirmed that a meeting was held in Union Quay RIC Barracks on 19 March 1920 between military and police officers to discuss the activities of MacCurtain and to plan his arrest for questioning.[23] During this meeting the military representatives produced evidence that MacCurtain had been present in Dublin in October 1919 when the Volunteers attempted to ambush the lord lieutenant, Lord French. The RIC refuted this suggestion, stating that he was in Cork on the date in question, but the military insisted their information was correct.[24] They later reconfirmed the evidence with their source, and then issued a dispatch ordering that the lord mayor be arrested for his treasonous activity. Feeley was told to deliver the dispatch to both County Inspector Maloney, at his room in the Metropole Hotel on King Street, and to District Inspector Swanzy, at his rooms in McTiernans' Hotel on St Patrick's Hill. The dispatch stated that the two police officers were to meet with the military party at St Luke's RIC Barracks and then proceed to MacCurtain's house in Blackpool. The fact that he was the elected lord mayor of the city provided him with no protection and, given the mentality of those who took the decision to arrest and/or kill him, it was probably considered an added bonus.

Tomás MacCurtain was killed in reprisal for the downward spiral of Volunteer attacks on the RIC. He was killed because he was the brigade commander of Cork No. 1 Brigade. He was killed in order to send a clear message to the nationalist population that no one was beyond the reach of the security forces. And the message to the Volunteers was unambiguous – cease the campaign of violence forthwith or face a similar fate. But this message was completely ignored and the violence continued.

MacCurtain's funeral mass took place at the North Cathedral on the morning of Monday, 22 March, and was attended by many prominent republicans from all over Ireland, together with the officers from Cork No. 1 Brigade. In a massive show of strength, uniformed Volunteers escorted the remains of their former commanding officer to his final resting place at St Fin Barre's cemetery. Delivering the graveside oration, Terence MacSwiney, who had now assumed command of Cork No. 1 Brigade, declared that: 'the great work that was being done by the lord mayor, though interrupted by his murder, would be carried on by the members of the Volunteer movement and no matter how many lost their lives in the course of their duty, as did MacCurtain, another would always be found to take the lead.'[25]

3

POLICE REINFORCEMENTS

Two days after MacCurtain's funeral, the RIC reinforcements recruited in Britain during January began arriving in Ireland. A shortage of police uniforms meant they ended up wearing a mixture of military service dress and green RIC uniforms. One of the first locations where the new constables were deployed was County Tipperary. At that time, Tipperary had a renowned pack of hounds known as the 'Black and Tans' and someone soon adopted the name for the new arrivals. The description stuck. When the first contingent arrived in Cork they were billeted in a house at Empress Place on Summerhill and greeted with posters distributed by the Volunteers which were anything but welcoming:

> Whereas the spies and traitors known as the Royal Irish Constabulary are holding this country for the enemy, and whereas said spies and bloodhounds are conspiring with the enemy to bomb and bayonet and otherwise outrage a peaceful, law abiding and liberty loving people.
>
> Whereas we do hereby proclaim and suppress said spies and traitors, and do hereby solemnly warn prospective recruits that they join the RIC at their own peril. All nations are agreed as to the fate of traitors. It has the sanction of God and man.[26]

By now Terence MacSwiney, acting on O'Donoghue's advice, had re-instated Seán O'Hegarty as brigade vice commandant. On 31

March, he was also elected lord mayor and in the course of his acceptance speech described himself, 'more as a soldier stepping into the breach, than as an administrator to fill the first post in the municipality'. Having paid tribute to his predecessor, he went on to point out that 'this contest of ours is not on our side a rivalry of vengeance but one of endurance – it is not they who can inflict most but they who can suffer most will conquer.'[27]

He also enunciated his military philosophy when he said that:

facing the enemy, we must declare our attitude simply. We see in their regime a thing of evil incarnate. With it there can be no parley, any more than there can be a truce with the powers of hell. This is our simple resolution. We ask for no mercy, and we will make no compromise. But to the divine author of mercy we appeal for strength to sustain us in our battle, whatever the persecution, that we may bring our people victory in the end.[28]

Three days later, on Easter Saturday, 3 April 1920, the first operation authorised under his command was carried out. The security forces expected a major Volunteer offensive to be launched nationally to coincide with the anniversary of the 1916 Rising and, in an effort to prevent this taking place, checkpoints were positioned on the roads leading into Dublin, Cork and Limerick. The expected offensive never materialised, but later that night, just before curfew, Volunteers throughout the country forced their way into almost 100 income tax offices and systematically burned all documents in them. They also burned 182 vacated RIC barracks to prevent them being reoccupied by the Black and Tans who were now pouring into the country. In Cork city, Volunteers successfully destroyed the income tax offices on South Mall and South Terrace and burned the evacuated RIC barracks at Togher.

Two weeks later, on 17 April, the inquest which had opened

on 20 March under Coroner James J. McCabe to investigate the circumstances surrounding MacCurtain's death concluded with the jury bringing in a verdict of 'wilful murder' against: David Lloyd George, prime minister of England; Lord French, lord lieutenant of Ireland; Ian MacPherson, former chief secretary of Ireland; Acting Inspector-General Smith of the RIC; Divisional Inspector Clayton of the RIC; District Inspector Swanzy and some unknown members of the RIC. While all of those mentioned clearly had a variety of questions to answer in relation to police policy and conduct on the night in question, Coroner McCabe was unable to specifically identify those who had actually killed the lord mayor. The only conclusion therefore which can be drawn with certainty is that several elements within the security forces held different and competing views on the threat which MacCurtain posed. On the night of 19 March one group went to arrest him, another went to kill him. His fate literally depended on who got there first, and the confusion generated before, during and after his murder conveniently facilitated a policy of denial which was subsequently adopted by everyone involved.

From this point onwards it became a Volunteer priority to identify those within the RIC who were responsible for killing MacCurtain. Florrie O'Donoghue, identified two individuals whom he thought had been involved – Sergeant Denis Garvey and Constable Daniel Harrington, who were both stationed in the RIC barracks on the Lower Road. MacSwiney, acting on O'Donoghue's advice, ordered Patrick 'Pa' Murray to eliminate them and having established that they usually took the tram into town after work, on the evening of 11 May, Murray deployed a four-man squad outside the RIC barracks. Two were positioned across the road in case the constables did not board the tram as anticipated, while Murray and Martin Donovan waited at the tram stop. When the tram approached, Garvey, Harrington and Constable Doyle left the barracks. Murray and Donovan boarded the tram first. When the RIC men entered the seating area the Volunteers opened fire, killing Garvey and Harrington and wounding Doyle.

MacCurtain's death had now been avenged in the sense that some RIC officers had been killed in reprisal but this was not the end of the matter. With the advent of summer, the Volunteer campaign escalated dramatically and on 14 May, the RIC barracks on the Commons Road, which had previously been evacuated, was burned to the ground.

On 3 June, a party of Volunteers under O'Donoghue's command attacked and destroyed the RIC barracks in Blarney. That same day the previously vacated barracks in Blackrock was also burned. On 1 July, the barracks on King Street was attacked, forcing the RIC to evacuate it. On 12 July, it was set alight, as were those at St Luke's and the Lower Road. On 14 July, the evacuated barracks on the Blackrock Road was destroyed by fire. Within a two-month period, seven barracks had been attacked and burned.

Of course none of this was happening in a political vacuum. On 23 March, three days after MacCurtain's death, Lloyd George offered General Sir Nevil Macready command of all British forces in Ireland and, on 29 March, he took up this appointment.[29] On 3 April, Ian MacPherson resigned as chief secretary and was replaced by Sir Hamar Greenwood, KC, the Liberal MP for Sunderland and under-secretary at the Home Office. Before taking up his appointment, on 30 April Greenwood stated optimistically that 'I go to Ireland as a friend of Ireland and I will do my best to bring peace' – but little did he know of the difficulties which lay ahead.[30]

When Greenwood eventually arrived in Dublin on 6 May, together with Sir Warren Fisher, Andrew Cope and two senior civil servants, he immediately set about examining the methodology of government employed by the administration in Dublin

Castle. A report subsequently prepared by Fisher, with a huge input from Cope, stated that the machinery of government and the administration's decision making process were completely obsolete. This resulted in the immediate appointment of Sir John Anderson, the chairman of the Board of Inland Revenue in London, as joint under-secretary with James MacMahon, while Andrew Cope replaced Sir John Taylor as assistant under-secretary.

Another new arrival to Ireland at this time was Major General Sir Henry H. Tudor who was appointed police advisor to the administration. Born in Exeter in 1871, Tudor was an experienced soldier whose primary duty was to take control and reorganise the police force in Ireland. One of his first innovations was the appointment of divisional commissioners to supervise and instruct county inspectors in the more military aspects of their duties.

In line with this policy, on 3 June, Lieutenant Colonel Gerald Bryce-Ferguson Smyth, a one-armed veteran of the King's Own Scottish Borderers who had been wounded six times in the First World War, was appointed divisional police commissioner for Munster. He immediately became embroiled in controversy. On 9 June, Smyth addressed police personnel at Listowel RIC Barracks and ordered them to adopt a hard-line 'shoot on sight' policy when dealing with known republican trouble-makers. Not everyone present agreed with this policy and Constable Jeremiah Mee resigned in protest on the spot. When senior officers then ordered that Mee be removed from the barracks his colleagues refused to act against him and the incident became known as the 'Listowel Mutiny'.

Eight days later, on 17 July, when Smyth was dining at the County Club on South Mall in the company of County Inspector Craig, six Volunteers commanded by Dan 'Sandow' O'Donovan stormed into the building and confronted the commissioner: 'Were not your orders to shoot on sight?' asked O'Donovan, 'Well, you are in our sights now, so prepare to die.'

The Volunteers then opened fire. Smyth was mortally wounded receiving two bullets to the head and three in the chest; Craig was more fortunate and received only a slight leg wound.

Once news of the attack began to circulate, a large crowd gathered on the street outside the County Club. When the security forces arrived to remove Smyth's body, a group of Black and Tans and some regular soldiers who were also present opened fire on the crowd in retaliation and forty people were wounded.

Responding to Smyth's death, Major General Strickland, officer commanding the 6th Division, issued the following curfew order on 20 July:

> I do hereby order and require every person within the area specified in the schedule hereto to remain within doors between the hours of 10 o'clock p.m. and 3 o'clock a.m., unless provided with a permit in writing from the competent military authority or some person duly authorised by him.
>
> Schedule – All the area within a radius of three miles of the General Post Office, Pembroke Street, in the city of Cork.
>
> Permits will be granted to clergymen, registered medical practitioners, and nurses engaged on urgent duties. Permits will not be granted to other persons save in the case of absolute necessity.
>
> Every person abroad between the hours mentioned in the foregoing order, when challenged by any policeman, or by an officer, N.C.O., or soldier on duty, must immediately halt and obey the orders given to him; and if he fails to do so, it will be at his own peril.[31]

The gloves were now off and troops from Victoria Barracks were detailed to enforce the order by conducting 'curfew patrols' across the city. In protest at this development, Cork Corporation decided to extinguish the street-lights during curfew hours which in turn made the city a sinister and very dangerous place by night. While these measures had an impact on the lives of ordinary people they had no curtailing effect whatever on the Volunteers who used the darkness and the shadows to move covertly and undetected through the city streets.

As the weeks wore on the preferred approach employed by the security forces was to deploy British army elements in support of the RIC. Although this tactic was used more and more frequently throughout the summer, Lloyd George refused to acknowledge that a state of war existed between Britain and Ireland. While the Volunteers considered themselves to be the army of the democratically elected government of the Irish people, the prime minister considered them to be nothing more that a gang of criminals and murderers who should be dealt with by the police. However RIC resignations continued to mount and the Black and Tans were proving to be largely ineffective and ill-disciplined. General Macready believed that:

> As policemen, they were useless. The value of a policeman lies in his knowledge of a locality and its inhabitants, of which the RIC recruits were necessarily ignorant. Nor could they obtain much help on these points from the old RIC with whom they served, because from some time past it had become necessary to move the police from place to place to prevent their becoming marked men in any particular locality.[32]

Upon taking over command in Ireland Macready had asked that eleven additional infantry battalions, together with service support units, be sent to Ireland as a matter of priority to combat the Volunteers. On 11 May, a cabinet meeting was held to discuss that subject. Sir Henry Wilson, the Chief of the Imperial General staff, later recorded in his diary that, 'the cabinet were frankly frightened, and agreed that all Macready's proposals [should] be acceded to'. Wilson, however, objected because any such deployment would leave insufficient forces to deal with any trouble that might erupt in Britain. It was eventually agreed that eight battalions be sent. Winston Churchill then suggested that instead of augmenting the military it might be preferable to raise a special force of 8,000 demobilised servicemen to reinforce the RIC. This was agreed in principle. The new force would be called the Auxiliary Division of the RIC, and enlistment would be open to former commissioned officers from the British armed forces.

Recruiting for the force opened on 12 July; the advertised wage was £1 a day with some allowances, and successful applicants were enrolled as 'temporary cadets' – a rank equivalent to that of sergeant in the RIC. The new recruits began to arrive in Ireland at the end of July and were sent to the Curragh where they underwent a six-week police course. Each new member was issued with a .45 Webley revolver and a .303 Lee Enfield rifle, and initially clothed in a British army officer pattern uniform with a green Tam-o-Shanter cap and RIC rank markings., However, they later acquired their own distinctive dark blue uniform with black leather accoutrements but retained the Tam-o-Shanter cap.

On 4 August, command of the Auxiliaries was given to Brigadier-General Frank Percy Crozier, CB, CMG, DSO, who quickly organised the 'Cadets' into alphabetically designated companies of 100 men to be deployed to the areas of greatest Volunteer activity. To ensure maximum mobility each company was equipped with two Ford armoured cars and six Crossley tenders. The first Auxiliaries were deployed into Cork county in August. In an effort to maintain the morale of the police – the British authorities in Dublin Castle also introduced a four-page publication entitled the *Weekly Summary*, the first issue of which appeared on 13 August

1920. This paper was issued free of charge to members of the RIC and DMP and gave a sanitised version of police operations. It also referred to the Volunteers as 'criminals' and 'murderers' and to their activities as 'the murder campaign'. For the hard-liners within the police who wanted to take the matter into their own hands this was exactly what they had been waiting for.

At this time a decision was also taken to implement new legislation to provide additional powers to the crown forces operating in Ireland. Since the outbreak of the war in January 1919, the British security forces had been trying to deal with Volunteer violence under the ordinary law of the land, supported by special powers granted to them under the terms of the Defence of the Realm Acts. However, by July 1920, General Macready felt that the legal framework within which he was expected to operate was insufficient to comprehensively deal with the situation in Ireland. Accordingly, he put forward a proposal to introduce Martial Law in Ireland. The British government refused to accede to his request but they did introduce a new piece of legislation known as the Restoration of Order in Ireland Act. This legislation received royal assent on 9 August and permitted the government to continue most of the restrictions imposed under the wartime Defence of the Realm Acts. However, it also permitted the commander-in-chief of British forces in Ireland to arrest and intern without trial anyone suspected of being a member of the Volunteer movement. In addition, it empowered courts-martial to try a wide range of offences including treason and felony.

The Act was also an opportunity to address the politically embarrassing situation being caused by the findings issued by coroners' inquests throughout Ireland. Up to that point thirty-three juries sitting in coroner's courts had indicted either the police or military for murder. To prevent this recurring, the Act suppressed these bodies and replaced them with military inquests. It soon transpired that Terence MacSwiney, MacCurtain's successor as lord mayor and officer commanding Cork No. 1 Brigade, would be the first person tried under the new legislation.

Ever since MacCurtain's election as lord mayor in January 1920, City Hall in Cork had come to symbolise republican resistance to British rule in the city. As well as being used for municipal affairs, the building was utilised by different republican organisations. On the night of 12 August, an important case was being heard before a republican court on the premises. That same night, Terence MacSwiney had summoned the members of his brigade council to a meeting in the building at 7.30 p.m. Unknown to either of these groups, a meeting of senior IRB officers was also scheduled to take place in the hall that night. A written notice for the latter meeting had been intercepted by British military intelligence and a decision was taken to act.

At 7.30 p.m., 300 troops and six armoured cars from Victoria Barracks approached City Hall. A cordon was thrown around the building and the troops stormed inside. Those found within were detained, and a detailed search of the premises got underway. Eventually most of the personnel found in the building were released around 9 p.m. but eleven people were arrested and taken to the Military Detention Barracks for questioning. In one swoop the security forces had captured the most influential Volunteer officers in Cork at that time: Terence MacSwiney, lord mayor of Cork city and OC, Cork No. 1 Brigade; Seán O'Hegarty, Vice OC, Cork No. 1 Brigade; Joseph O'Connor, Quartermaster, Cork No. 1 Brigade; Daniel O'Donovan, OC 1st Battalion, Cork No. 1 Brigade; Michael Leahy, OC 4th Battalion, Cork No. 1 Brigade; Liam Lynch, OC, Cork No. 2 Brigade; Patrick McCarthy, Michael Carey, Laurence Cotter, Thomas Mulcahy and Patrick Harris.

When they arrived at the Military Detention Barracks, Terence MacSwiney was stripped of all his possessions with the exception of his chain of office which he refused to hand over. In protest at their arrest, MacSwiney and the others announced that they would be joining the republican prisoners in Cork Gaol who had already commenced a hunger strike on 11 August to highlight the fact that they were being detained without trial. With the exception of MacSwiney, the other ten detainees had all given false names and the following morning they were transferred to Cork Gaol. Three days later, in what must rate as one of the greatest failures of British intelligence during the entire conflict, all ten were released. On Monday, 16 August, MacSwiney was taken back to Victoria Barracks where he found a court-martial waiting for him. He was charged on the following four counts:

1. Without lawful authority or excuse being in possession of a cypher, on August 12, which cypher being the numerical cypher issued to the R.I.C.
2. Having this cypher under his control.
3. Being in possession of documents, the publication of which would be likely to cause disaffection to his majesty. [This document was the resolution passed by the Corporation acknowledging the authority of, and pledging allegiance to, Dáil Éireann.]
4. Being in possession of a copy of the speech the lord mayor made when elected as successor to Tomás MacCurtain.

When asked if he wished to be represented by counsel, MacSwiney declared the court to be 'illegal' and said that those who took part were 'liable to arrest under the laws of the Irish Republic'. He then informed the court that it was a grave offence to commit any act against the head of a city and he dismissed the charges laid against him. He concluded by drawing their attention to the fact that, 'seized among my papers was a copy of a letter I addressed to his Holiness the Pope on the occasion of the beatification of Oliver

Plunkett. His Holiness has read that letter by now, and it will be of interest to him to learn that this is a seditious document when found in my possession'.[33]

Having heard MacSwiney, the members of the court retired and, after fifteen minutes, returned to announce their verdict. The lord mayor was found not guilty on the first charge but guilty on the second, third and fourth. When the verdict was announced MacSwiney addressed the court one more time: 'I wish to state that I will put a limit to any term of imprisonment you may impose, because of the action I will take. I have taken no food since Thursday, therefore I will be free in a month'.[34] He was then sentenced to two years imprisonment and, in the early hours of the following morning, he was transferred to Pembroke in South Wales and then on to London where he was incarcerated in Brixton Prison.

4

O'HEGARTY TAKES COMMAND

With MacSwiney behind bars in England, political power in Cork city now passed to Dónal O'Callaghan, the deputy lord mayor.[35] However, and more importantly, command of Cork No. 1 Brigade passed into the hands of the brigade vice-commandant, Seán O'Hegarty.[36] This move now placed the control of both the Volunteers and IRB in Cork city into the hands of one man. Appalled at MacSwiney's treatment, and still hurting from Mac-Curtain's murder, O'Hegarty's succession brought with it a legacy of frustration which had been at boiling point for a long time. This frustration was now about to erupt violently in the face of the British authorities who would have to deal with a far more volatile adversary – whom they had previously banished from the city. And erupt it did. The first major operation planned, approved, and executed by O'Hegarty was the elimination of District Inspector Oswald Swanzy, the man believed to have been most responsible for the death of Tomás MacCurtain.

In the wake of MacCurtain's death, the RIC leadership decided to transfer Swanzy and a number of other prominent members of the force from the city for their own safety. The Volunteers eventually tracked Swanzy to Lisburn, County Antrim and a decision was taken to execute him. O'Hegarty sent Seán Culhane and Dick Murphy to Dublin to meet with Michael Collins and Cathal Brugha and once Collins had agreed to the operation, Culhane, Murphy, Leo 'Stetto' Ahern, Jack Coady and Christy MacSwiney were tasked to carry out the killing. The group made their way to Belfast where they linked up with Roger McCorley of the Belfast Brigade who had already carried out a detailed surveillance on Swanzy and was familiar with his movements. Culhane brought with him MacCurtain's revolver and it was prearranged that the first shot fired at Swanzy would be from this weapon. At 1.06 p.m. on the afternoon of 22 August the Corkmen opened fire on Swanzy as he left Christ Church Cathedral in Lisburn and shot him dead.

There had been no due process for MacCurtain and there was no due process for Swanzy either – such was the nature of the conflict that now engulfed Ireland. However, aside from the Volunteers' belief that Swanzy had been behind the murder of the lord mayor, there was in fact no physical evidence which placed the RIC inspector at MacCurtain's house the night he was killed. This was of no concern to O'Hegarty. As far as he was concerned, MacCurtain's death was avenged and he immediately turned his attention to the fate of Terence MacSwiney, who was by now on the nineteenth day of his hunger strike. A special meeting of the brigade staff was held in the home of the Wallace sisters at which it was decided that an attempt would be made to capture Major General Strickland and then hold him hostage to obtain MacSwiney's release.

Strickland regularly had to travel to England on military business. On these occasions a touring car would take both him and his aide-de-camp (ADC) from Victoria Barracks to Penrose Quay via Sidney Hill, Wellington Road, St Patrick's Hill and MacCurtain Street. On arrival at the quay he would board the passenger steamer, the S.S. *Bandon*, which usually left Cork at 5.30 p.m. each evening.

It was decided that the attempt to capture Strickland would be made as his car slowed down at the bottom of St Patrick's Hill before turning left on to what was now MacCurtain Street (previously King Street). O'Hegarty would command the operation himself. Michael Kenny, a member of the brigade intelligence squad who could positively identify Strickland and the car in which he usually travelled, was ordered to take up a position at the junction of Wellington Road and St Patrick's Hill to act as the scout. Other Volunteers, armed with revolvers and led by O'Hegarty, would take up positions on the footpath at the bottom of the hill and, when Kenny observed Strickland's car coming down Wellington Road, he would alert them using a prearranged signal. Volunteers James and Jeremiah Grey, would jump onto the running board on the driver's side, and force him to stop the vehicle. O'Hegarty and the others would rush the car and transfer the general and any other officers that were with him into two waiting cars which were to be driven to a shack located in a remote part of the country, west of Ballincollig. Strickland's driver and his ADC would be detained in the general's car and taken to a different location.

Soon after this decision was taken O'Hegarty and his men took their positions. The plan was that they would remain in position until 6 p.m. each evening after which time the S.S. *Bandon* would have sailed for England. But several days passed and there was no sign of Strickland.

In the meantime, another group of Cork Volunteers had departed for London with instructions from Collins to assassinate members of the British cabinet if MacSwiney actually died. Pa Murray, Jack Coady and Con Collins had made contact with Sam Maguire and Reggie Dunne of the London Volunteers and were actively involved in monitoring the activities of different ministers.

Murray later recalled that:

Things proceeded slowly for about six weeks. Meanwhile, I acquainted myself with the streets where these ministers were living, and the routes they might possibly take to and from the House of Commons … we discovered after a time that the movements of the ministers were most irregular and uncertain and, for that reason, I was not able to devise any definite plan to carry out my objective should the occasion arise … the strain [of this work] was very severe on the three of us and we were coming to the stage where anything might happen to ourselves or in the work we had undertaken.[37]

When Collins sent confirmation that some action should be taken if MacSwiney died Murray informed him that he had definite information that Arthur Balfour would be in Oxford on a particular day and that he would attempt to shoot him whether MacSwiney was alive or dead. However, Collins refused to sanction the attack on that basis. Nevertheless, Murray went to Oxford as planned and actually met his target on the street:

I simply walked up to him and asked him the way to some of the Oxford colleges. He directed me and said, 'You are an Irishman?' I said, 'Yes', and he walked a bit of the way with me. He did not appear to have an armed guard with him. I returned to Dublin on the following Thursday. Michael Collins told me he was sorry, but that he could not risk anything happening until Terence died. He also felt that the strain on us would be too much, if MacSwiney were to die while we were in England.[38]

In Cork on Friday, 24 September, the opportunity O'Hegarty had been waiting for finally presented itself. At 5.45 p.m. Kenny caught sight of Strickland's car making its way down Wellington Road in the evening traffic. All the occupants were dressed in civilian clothes, the general's ADC sat in front next to the driver, and Strickland was in the back seated between another staff officer and Captain James Kelly. Kenny immediately tried to alert the

Grey brothers but he failed to attract their attention. As the car turned left onto St Patrick's Hill, Kenny continued to signal but his efforts were in vain. In desperation he pulled out his revolver and ran after the car hoping to jump onto the running board himself but the staff officer in the rear of the car saw him chasing them and alerted the driver while drawing his own revolver. The driver increased speed in an attempt to drive out of danger and as the car pulled away Kenny began shooting. The officers in the rear of the car returned fire, and the sound of the shots finally alerted O'Hegarty and the others who also drew their revolvers and opened fire.

With pedestrians scattering in all directions a close-quarters gun fight got underway. The driver of the car was wounded but succeeded in getting his vehicle on to MacCurtain Street, in spite of the fact that both the windscreen and side windows were shattered. Bullets also smashed into the windows of a number of nearby shops and one civilian was wounded in the forearm. As the car careered down MacCurtain Street it collided with a tram-way pole but managed to stay on the road. Although the Volunteers chased it half-way down the street it was clear Strickland could not now be caught and O'Hegarty ordered his men to disperse.

That same day, MacSwiney wrote the following letter to O'Hegarty:

Seán,

A last line in case I don't return – I want to bid you god speed for the future, and it sends me back on the past. Do you remember the first drill in the Dún under Goodwin when we took the floor eight strong? I was in the first square, and I think you were. We had many vicissitudes together since and much good work for the Republic. How happy it is to recall the wonderful progress. I pray, Seán that you may be spared long to carry on the good work – to come safely through the Battle and live in the hour of victory. I am very weary and must stop.

Goodbye Seán. God bless you and give you a long life under the free Republic.

> Your old comrade,
> Terry.[39]

His hunger strike and those of the Volunteers incarcerated in Cork Gaol were now attracting world wide interest and sympathy. On 17 October 1920, Michael Fitzgerald, commandant of the 1st Battalion, Cork No. 2 Brigade, passed away in Cork Gaol on his sixty-seventh day without food. Eight days later, on 25 October, Joseph Murphy, a seventeen year old Volunteer from Cork No. 1 Brigade also died in Cork Gaol on the seventy-sixth day of his hunger strike. On that same morning, Terence MacSwiney finally passed away in Brixton Prison having refused food for seventy-four days. As the city of Cork mourned the death of yet another lord mayor, Dónal O'Callaghan, the deputy lord mayor, issued the following defiant statement on 26 October:

> The republican hold on the municipal chair of Cork ceases only when the last republican in Cork has followed Tomás MacCurtain and Terence MacSwiney into the grave. Murder will not terrorise us.[40]

The requiem mass for Michael Fitzgerald was held on the morning of 19 October at the church of SS Peter and Paul's. After the mass, crown forces with steel helmets and fixed bayonets entered the church and served notice on the priest that only 100 persons would be allowed in the cortège. Despite this warning, and the fact that armoured cars and lorries full of troops had been positioned around the entrance to the church, thousands of people took part in the funeral procession through the city streets as the remains began their final journey to Kilcrumper cemetery near Fermoy where Fitzgerald was buried with full military honours. Joseph Murphy also received full military honours when he was laid to rest in the republican plot in St Fin Barre's cemetery on 27 October. When MacSwiney's remains arrived in Cork city around 4 p.m. on 31 October they were taken to City Hall where they lay in state overnight. The following morning they were taken to the North Cathedral and, after a requiem mass attended by political, civic and religious dignitaries from all over Ireland, they were also taken to St Fin Barre's cemetery, where they were laid to rest alongside Tomás MacCurtain and Joseph Murphy.

5

Killings and Burnings

Five days before MacSwiney's death the British foreign secretary stood up in the House of Commons and informed the members that between 1 January 1919 and 18 October 1920 the Volunteers had destroyed 64 courthouses, 492 vacated RIC barracks, 21 occupied RIC barracks and 148 private residences belonging to citizens loyal to the crown. He also informed the House that a further 114 RIC barracks had been damaged, there had been 741 raids on the mail service, 40 attacks on coastguard stations and light-houses, 117 policemen had been killed, 185 policemen wounded, 23 British soldiers killed, 71 soldiers wounded, 32 civilians killed and wounded.

These statistics were staggering but they failed to tell the whole story. What the foreign secretary conveniently forgot to mention was the scale of destruction and damage to property being visited upon entire communities by crown forces engaged in punitive and unauthorised retaliatory operations. The first of these actions had occurred in Fermoy on the night of 8 September 1919 when soldiers from the King's Shropshire Light Infantry Regiment attacked a number of shops in retaliation for an ambush carried out the previous day. The next major reprisal occurred in Midleton when serious damage was inflicted on the town on the night of 5 June 1920. This reprisal was in the aftermath of an operation carried out by Volunteers from Cork No. 1 Brigade under Commandant Diarmuid Hurley when a cycle patrol of twelve Cameron Highlanders had been disarmed.

Tuam in County Galway suffered a similar fate on the night of 19–20 July when, following the killing of two RIC constables in an ambush at nearby Aughle, the Black and Tans rampaged through the streets burning the town hall and a number of other buildings.

Then, on 20 July, a group of Auxiliaries from Gormanstown shot dead two local men and burned a factory and a number of houses in Balbriggan, County Dublin, after the Volunteers had shot dead Head Constable Peter Burke and wounded his brother, Sergeant Michael Burke, in a public house in the village.

Tipperary town was sacked on 30 July after two soldiers from the Oxfordshire Regiment were killed and three others wounded when their lorry was ambushed at Oola, County Limerick.

On the night of 22 September, the towns of Ennistymon, Lahinch and Milltown Malbay in County Clare were all sacked, and six local men were killed, after a major engagement had been fought between crown forces and members of the Mid-Clare Brigade at Rineen, near Milltown Malbay, earlier in the day.

Five days later, on 27 September, the town of Trim, County Meath, was ransacked by over 200 Black and Tans and Auxiliaries after the Volunteers had earlier attacked and captured the local RIC barracks. The following day a unit of Volunteers from Cork No. 2 Brigade attacked and occupied the military barracks in Mallow while the majority of the garrison from the 17th Lancers were out of barracks exercising their horses. A sergeant from the Lancers was shot dead during the operation in which the Volunteers confiscated an arsenal of weapons and ammunition. That night troops from the military barracks at Buttevant and Fermoy descended on Mallow and, as Florence O'Donoghue later wrote, they:

Set about the business of burning and looting public and private property in an organised military operation. They created a night of terror for the inhabitants of the town. The local creamery and the town hall were burned to the ground. Drunken troops roamed the streets, firing indiscriminately and throwing petrol-filled bottles into any house that showed a light.[41]

The situation was spiralling out of control and it attracted adverse publicity in most of the British press. On 24 September, the editorial in the *Daily News* in London stated that, 'The suspicion is rapidly growing in this country and abroad that British authority is secretly conniving at the barbarous reprisals now being systematically and openly carried out in Ireland.' Three days later, a letter penned by General Sir Herbert Gough appeared in the *Manchester Guardian* in which he said, 'I don't think any truthful or sane person can avoid the conclusion that the authorities are deliberately encouraging and, what is more, actually screening reprisals and 'counter-terror by armed forces of the crown'. The issue of reprisals by crown forces operating in Ireland was also causing some concern to Field Marshal Sir Henry Wilson who met with Lloyd George and Bonar Law, the leader of the Conservative party, on 29 September, to discuss the matter. That night he recorded what occurred in his diary:

I had one and a half hours this evening with Lloyd George and Bonar Law. I told them what I thought of reprisals by the 'Black and Tans', and how this must lead to chaos and ruin. Lloyd George danced about and was angry, but I never budged. I pointed out that these reprisals were carried out without anyone being responsible; men were murdered, houses burnt, villages wrecked (such as Balbriggan, Ennistymon, Trim, etc.). I said that this was due to want of discipline, and this must be stopped. It was the business of the government to govern. If these men ought to be murdered, then the government ought to murder them. Lloyd George danced at all this, said no government could possibly take this responsibility. After much wrangling, I still sticking to it that either these things ought to be done or ought not, and if they ought then it was the business of the government to do them, and if they ought not then they ought to be stopped, I got some sense into their heads, and Lloyd George wired for Hamar Greenwood, Macready, Tudor and others to come over tomorrow night. I warned Lloyd George that, although up to now the army had remained disciplined and quiet, it was quite possible that they might break out any minute if one of their officers were murdered by Sinn Féiners, and that the report tonight that Mallow had been sacked after the murder of one of the sergeants of the 17th Lancers may well prove that the 17th Lancers had sacked the town. All this was terribly dangerous. What was evident to me after this long talk was that neither Lloyd George nor Bonar Law had the faintest idea of what to do.[42]

Throughout the summer of 1920, Cork city had been spared reprisal attacks by crown forces. All that now began to change as a direct consequence of the hard-line influence of Seán O'Hegarty, who authorised the establishment of the Cork city active service unit (ASU) during the month of September 1920. This unit, which consisted of sixteen to twenty full time Volunteers, were paid £6 a week and could be reinforced from the local Volunteer companies. Commanded by Pa Murray, the ASU operated in teams of four with two 'front men' and two 'back-up men'. The quality of intelligence now being provided to the Cork No. 1 Brigade by Florrie O'Donoghue also began to have an impact.

The first casualty in this new phase of the conflict was Seán O'Callaghan, who was abducted by the Volunteers from his home at 13 Pickets Lane on Bandon Road in Cork city on 15 September.

Two days later he was charged with being an informer based on evidence produced by O'Donoghue, and executed soon thereafter.

On the evening of 27 September, in an operation that was probably a reprisal for O'Callaghan's abduction and death, a bomb explosion destroyed the premises of the Castle & Co. shop near the Cork Arcade and ten other buildings in the vicinity sustained serious fire and structural damage. A joint RIC/British army patrol claimed they had been attacked by members of the Volunteers who had thrown a bomb and then fired upon them. However newspaper reports the following day cited witnesses who disputed this version of events and denied that any Volunteers were involved. Clearly there were now different versions of the truth and this spelled very bad news for the population at large who would soon find themselves trapped in the middle.

This became evident at 12.35 a.m. on the morning of 3 October when Volunteers from Cork No. 1 Brigade took up positions in the Blackthorn House on St Patrick's Street and opened fire on a party of Black and Tans as they passed by. Three were wounded and Constable Clarence Victor Chave later died from his wounds in the military hospital at Victoria Barracks.[43]

Five days later, on Friday, 8 October, the Volunteers struck again, this time ambushing a British army lorry travelling along Barrack Street. One soldier was killed in this incident and three others were wounded.[44]

At 3.45 a.m. the following morning, Saturday, 9 October, in what was now unequivocally an urban guerrilla war, a group of unidentified men set fire to City Hall. Were it not for the prompt arrival of Cork Fire Brigade, under the command of Captain Alfred Hutson, the whole building would have been destroyed. Nevertheless, serious damage was still done to the western side of the building which housed the offices of the health department and waterworks.

Cork Corporation Fire Brigade had been formed by the city

fathers back in October 1877 with Mark Wickham as superintendent. The first fire station in the city was situated in the municipal offices on South Mall but was later transferred to Sullivan's Quay. In the wake of a major fire that destroyed the courthouse on Washington Street on 27 March 1891, the corporation demoted Wickham to brigade foreman and replaced him with Alfred Hutson.

Born in London on 14 April 1849, Hutson had served as a fireman with the Metropolitan Fire Brigade in London and as station officer with Brighton Fire Brigade. He held the latter position until August 1891 when he moved to Cork to take up the appointment of superintendent. Hutson was an experienced fire-fighter and an able administrator. In 1894, he succeeded in having a new fire station built on Sullivan's Quay and was instrumental in having a second station built at Grattan Street shortly afterwards.

The only means of escape from a fire at this time was by using wheeled escaped ladders that were brought to the scene by firemen. These ladders were housed in 'escape stations' situated at strategic locations throughout the city. While Wickham had introduced a number of such stations, Hutson increased them until by 1920 there was one situated at Sullivan's Quay, Grattan Street, Lavitt's Quay, Shandon Street, at the toll box at St Luke's Cross and one near Fr Mathew's statue on St Patrick's Street. All these escape stations were unmanned except the one on St Patrick's Street and an 'outstation' or hut was erected near the statue to serve as accommodation for the fireman who took up duty there in the evenings.[45] The only fire-fighting equipment Hutson had at his disposal in 1920 was one Merryweather steam pump that had been purchased in 1905, a motor fire tender that was used to carry ladders and other equipment, and a number of horse drawn hose reels. and all of these were used successfully to put out the fire in City Hall on 9 October.

Four days after the fire, on 13 October, in a new development, the following letter appeared in the *Cork Examiner*:

Anti-Sinn Féin Society
Circle Headquarters,
Grand Parade
Cork.

To: The Editor *Cork Constitution*, *Examiner* and *Evening Echo*,
copy to Canon Cohalan, Bandon.

Gentlemen,
I am instructed by the Supreme Council of the All Ireland Anti-Sinn Féin Society (Cork Circle) to request that you will be good enough to give publicity to the following decision which this organisation has reluctantly come to as the result of the present campaign of assassination being waged against members of his Majesty's forces in this country. My society desires it to be known that their object is to stop murders and not in any way to interfere with the aspirations of the people. By publishing this letter numerous lives may be saved.

DECISION
At a specially convened meeting of the All Ireland Anti-Sinn Féin Society held in Cork on this 11th day of October, 1920, we, the Supreme Council of the Cork Circle have reluctantly decided that – If, in the future any of his Majesty's forces be murdered – TWO members of the Sinn Féin Party in the county of Cork will be killed and in the event of a member of the Sinn Féin Party not being available three sympathisers will be killed. This will apply equally to laity and clergy of all denominations. In the event of a member of his Majesty's forces being wounded or an attempt being made to wound him ONE member of the Sinn Féin Party will be killed, or if

a member of the Sinn Féin Party is not available TWO sympathisers will be killed – I have the honour to subscribe myself, yours truly, The Assistant Secretary.

The publication of this letter raised a number of questions: what was the Anti-Sinn Féin Society? Who were its members? Whom did it represent? Was it to be taken seriously? In fact, it was not possible to answer any of these questions. While there was a strong loyalist minority in the city, it was not conceivable that these people had either the incentive or the means to threaten execution on anyone who held opposing views. A better interpretation suggests that this was both a deception plan and black propaganda by some elements within the British security forces. It was probably designed to convince the public that a body of opinion opposed to Volunteer activity actually existed, and thereby, serve as a deterrent – and also provide a plausible cover-story for future reprisals.

The Labour opposition was now extremely unhappy with the way security in Ireland was being administered. Through its deputy leader, Arthur Henderson, they tabled the following motion in the House of Commons on 20 October:

That this House regrets the present state of lawlessness in Ireland and the lack of discipline in the armed forces of the Crown, resulting in the death and injury of innocent civilians and the destruction of property; and is of the opinion that an independent investigation should be at once instituted into the causes, nature and extent of reprisals on the part of those whose duty is the maintenance of law and order.[46]

Henderson went on to express the opinion that, 'the distressing and deplorable situation existing in Ireland constituted a most humiliating and damaging indictment of the administrative policy of the ministers'. He said there appeared to be 'a policy of military terrorism which is not only a betrayal of democratic principles but is totally opposed to the best traditions of the British people, and is akin to the policy of frightfulness usually associated with the Huns'. Having expressed his 'outrage and abhorrence' at the actions carried out by 'Sinn Féiners' he said he believed it was the 'repressive policy of the government' that led to these 'outrages' and that the reprisals appeared to be 'a deliberate and calculated effort to destroy the Irish nationalist political movement'.

In reply, Hamar Greenwood said that Irish nationalists had nothing to do with the present difficulties and, further, there had been no reprisals against them. He also stated that the information Henderson had supplied to the House came from the 'headquarters of the Irish Republican Army which had within its ranks the assassins who were killing the loyal servants of the crown'. He said the House had to make up its mind whether it would accept this information or information provided by the chief secretary. Greenwood then said that, based on 'official knowledge', there was a 'highly organised propaganda movement that could be said, regardless of fact, to smirch the name of the United Kingdom and the legal servants of the crown'.

He told the members that the vast majority of Irish people hoped and prayed for the cessation of the 'outrages' being carried out by the Irish Republican Army. He was glad to inform them that the forces of the crown were breaking the terror in Ireland. He carried on by saying that, 'British soldiers and British police were not to be condemned if they fired first at the people who were trying to ambush them and annihilate them.' He would support them and he trusted the House would also support them as they were fighting a 'gang of terrorists – not ordinary decent, gentle, good-natured Irishmen'.

Greenwood also referred to a previous statement by Herbert

Asquith who had compared the village of Balbriggan after Auxi-liaries had sacked it to a Belgian town on the frontier in the First World War. In reply, Greenwood vigorously refuted the comparison, declaring that, while he more than anyone else had the right to regret what happened at Balbriggan, because, 'it did mean a certain break in the splendid discipline of the Irish police', the statement had no relation to the facts. Having informed the members of the House of the details surrounding the death of Head Constable Burke and the wounding of his brother, Greenwood then said that when the Auxiliaries saw their bodies 'they saw red – I admit it with regret. I always view these actions with the profoundest regret. In Balbriggan that night nineteen houses of Sinn Féiners were destroyed or damaged, four public houses were destroyed, and one hosiery factory'.

He also admitted that having made the 'fullest inquiry' into the case he found that, 'from 100 to 150 men went to Balbriggan determined to avenge the death of a popular comrade shot at and murdered in cold blood', but that he found it impossible out of the 150 to find the men who had done the deed.

Speaking in favour of the motion Herbert Asquith declared that while he recognised it was the duty of the military and police to defend themselves, the reason the motion was put forward was because there was *primae facie* evidence that in not a few instances the officers and servants of the executive had gone far beyond the limits of legitimate self-defence and had engaged in a campaign of outrage against unoffending and innocent people.

Responding to this, Greenwood informed the House that:

the military and police upon which we have to rely, should feel that the government, the House of Commons and the people were behind them ... The reason why the government will not have an inquiry was that they did not intend the soldiers and police could have any doubt that they would back them in every legitimate way. Anything in the nature of reprisals was a deadly thing because it invariably weakened the discipline of the force. The government will have the cases inquired into but the police and soldiers would know that the inquiry would be undertaken fairly by people who realised their responsibilities and dangers and not an inquiry which would be held by their enemies. The issue is clear. Here is this great murder conspiracy which only a few months ago many people were telling the government would beat them unless they gave way to it. One body of opinion represented by Mr Asquith said they must surrender to crime. Another body of opinion represented by the prime minister and myself think peace will never be accrued by such a surrender. We are determined that whatever is given to Ireland will be given as a result of calm consideration of what is just and fair, and there will be no party to giving anything as a concession to murder.[47]

A number of other members also spoke in favour of Henderson's motion calling for an independent inquiry into events in Ireland but the motion was defeated by 346 votes to 79. Completely frustrated with this result the Labour Party decided to establish its own commission, under the chairmanship of Henderson to inquire into republican violence and security force reprisals.[48]

Significantly, while the members of this commission were preparing for their task, a similar body called the 'American Commission on Conditions in Ireland' held its first public meeting in Washington DC on 19 November under the chairmanship of L. Hollingsworth Wood. In an effort to ensure complete impartiality they sent out invitations to representatives from all shades of religious and political opinion in Ireland asking them to attend and give evidence.[49] The invitees included Sir Edward Carson, Lord French and Sir Hamar Greenwood but there was no reply from any of them, nor indeed from any representative of the unionist community.

Oswald Swanzy's sister did indicate that she was prepared to travel and attend but she subsequently sent word that 'certain information she had received from sources unnamed had caused her to change her mind'. However Terence MacSwiney's widow, Muriel, his sister, Mary, and Susanna and Anna Walsh, the sisters-in-law of Tomás MacCurtain, did give evidence – as did the lord mayor, Dónal O'Callaghan, even though he had to travel to the United States as a stowaway.

However the commission had no impact on events in Ireland and in Cork, on 29 October, Volunteers from the Coachford Company of the Seventh Battalion captured two Royal Artillery officers named Brown and Rutherford near Macroom. According to Charlie Brown, the battalion adjutant, these men were dressed in 'civilian clothes', 'were armed with revolvers and also carried cameras'. The two officers were transferred to the Rusheen Company area for interrogation and subsequently executed as enemy spies.[50] Much later the British army did admit that both Brown and Rutherford had been employed from time to time on intelligence work'.[51]

With Volunteer violence escalating and reprisals having little or no impact General Crozier took the decision to form a new company of Auxiliary cadets and station them in Cork city. This unit would become known as K Company and Crozier later recalled how it was established:

I formed the company in November by taking a platoon from each of three other companies without warning the company commanders (so that they should not 'pack' their 'duds' into the new company). We had come down to a three company establishment, as we had done with battalions in France in 1918 in brigades, in order to get a greater number of smaller units into the field. The men were not 'new men' as they had all served together in other companies elsewhere.[52]

K Company was placed under the command of thirty four year old Colonel Owen William R. G. Latimer, a retired Royal Air Force officer. Colonel Latimer and the first Auxillaries began to arrive in the city in October and, due to a shortage of accommodation, they were billeted in the gymnasium at Victoria Barracks. As officer accommodation in the barracks was very scarce at the time when he arrived, Latimer took a room at the Imperial Hotel on the South Mall.

The arrival of the new Auxiliaries failed to discourage the Volunteers and, on 6 November, two Auxiliary intelligence officers based in Macroom were abducted. Cadets Bertram Agnew and Lionel R. Mitchell were in Johnson and Perrott's motor garage at Emmet Place when they were captured. They were subsequently taken to a secret location, interrogated, and shot dead.[53]

On 9 November, Lloyd George addressed the worsening situation in Ireland. Speaking at the Lord Mayor's banquet at London's Guildhall, he said:

There is no doubt that at last their [the crown forces] patience has given way and that there has been some severe hitting back ... Let us be fair to these gallant men who are doing their duty in Ireland ... It is no use talking about these being reprisals when these things are being done [by the Volunteers] in Ireland. We have murder by the throat ... When the government was ready we struck the terrorists and now the terrorists are complaining of terror.

The following day in the course of a search operation being conducted by the Auxiliaries at Tourindubh, near Ballingeary,

Volunteer Christopher Lucey from Cork No. 1 Brigade was discovered hiding in a 'safe house'. When the Auxiliaries called upon Lucey to surrender, he opened fire on them and was shot dead. His remains were brought back to Cork city and were buried in St Fin Barre's cemetery.

However, tension in the city did ease somewhat on 12 November when the remaining nine prisoners in Cork Gaol, now on the ninety-fourth day of their hunger strike, called off their protest after receipt of a letter from Arthur Griffith. In it Griffith said: 'I am of the opinion that our countrymen in Cork prison have sufficiently proved their devotion and fidelity and that they should now, as they were prepared to die for Ireland, prepare to live for her'.[54]

In England, it emerged that a group called the Anti-Reprisal Association had been founded on 10 November by a number of prominent members of the British establishment. These gentlemen were so concerned about the situation in Ireland, and the government's apparent apathy, that they gathered in London to lobby MPs to end the practice of 'unofficial reprisals'. The executive of this group included Commander Kenworthy, MP, G. K. Chesterson, Sir J. E. Swinburne-Harman and the Reverend H. Rylatt.

Despite this development, Sir Henry Wilson noted in his diary that same night that the situation in Ireland was not causing any particular concern to Lloyd George, or the other members of the government:

A cabinet [meeting] on Ireland [was held]. I was not sent for, but they thought that everything was going on so well in Ireland, i.e. government by 'Black and Tans'. They [decided] that they would leave it at that and not take over reprisals by government action.[55]

6

SPIES, INFORMERS AND REPRISALS

But everything was not 'going on so well' in Ireland. On 12 November, Sir Henry Tudor, police advisor to the British administration in Ireland, found it necessary to write a memorandum to all RIC constables assuring them of his fullest support 'in the most drastic action against the band of assassins, the so-called IRA'. He went on to say that:

> these murderers must be pursued relentlessly and their organisation ruthlessly suppressed. The initiative must be seized, the ambushers must be ambushed. The leaders and members of the criminal gang are mostly known to us. They must be given no rest. They must be hunted down. But, for the effectual performance of these duties, the highest discipline is essential.[56]

However, Tudor's memorandum came too late. Discipline within the RIC was already breaking down and the situation nationwide had now effectively developed into outright war where information was gathered, processed, and then acted upon violently by both sides. This was particularly true in Cork where Florrie O'Donoghue had successfully penetrated the security structures at Victoria Barracks: Pat Margetts, an Irish soldier serving in the barracks, was a republican sympathiser; Volunteer Michael Kenny, a French polisher by trade, was often employed in the barracks; and Volunteer Con Conroy, a former member of the royal navy, was employed there as a civilian clerk in the barrack adjutants' office where he had access to high quality information. But without doubt O'Donoghue's greatest asset in the barracks was Josephine Brown, a young war widow who was employed as a forewoman clerk in the registry office of the headquarters of the 6th Division. In this capacity, she was in charge of twenty-five clerks and had direct access to most of the confidential orders and reports that were received and issued from divisional headquarters. The couple had been introduced to one another in September by Fr Dominic O'Connor and had quickly developed a personal and covert relationship. Thereafter Brown risked her life on a daily basis to smuggle out copies of high value documentation while O'Donoghue in turn channelled the information into the planning of Volunteer operations.[57]

Brown later recalled:

Under the direction of the Brigade Officers, I paid special attention to securing information with regard to personnel and movements of the British Intelligence Staff attached to the 6th division and transmitted a list of the other officers of the staff. As I brought out and passed on to the Brigade IO much other material in cases where several copies of a document were made in the offices, including on one occasion a general order issued by General Strickland relating to general policy and tactics to be used by his forces in seeking out and attacking IRA columns … Where it was not possible to get copies I made shorthand notes of important documents, or on such points as appeared to be of special value. In other cases I took the actual letters after they had been made up for the post, and passed them over to the Brigade IO. These were opened and copied, and then put back into the next day's post by me.[58]

An early example of how this relationship worked saw Brown pass high-grade information to O'Donoghue in relation to the movements of three British intelligence officers. She had discovered that Captain M. H. W. Green, education officer with the 6th Division, Lieutenant Chambers, education officer 17th Brigade, and Lieutenant W. Watts of 33rd Field Company, Royal Engineers, were scheduled to leave Cork on 17 November on the 9.45 a.m. train to travel to Bere Island on the Bandon and South Coast Railway. When this information was passed to O'Donoghue, it was quickly decided that it was too good an opportunity to ignore. An operation was planned, and several members of the Cork No. 1 Brigade boarded the train in civilian attire. The three British officers also boarded with Watts travelling in the first-class carriage and the other two purchasing third-class seats to be less conspicuous. Lieutenant Goode, an inspector of army schools, was also on the train and he described what happened next:

> The first stop occurred at Waterfall, 8 miles out. The train had been standing for about half a minute. We were travelling in a third class carriage in which there were ten people altogether. We were in plain clothes. Three men [also] in plain clothes entered the compartment and the leading man walked across to the far side and the other two stood in the gangway. When the leading man reached the opposite door he turned, threw aside his overcoat exposing a Webley revolver in his right hand resting on his thigh. He said 'Hands up' and then 'Hands up all of ye'. I then saw the other two had revolvers in their hands ... the middle man then looked round the compartment and pointing to Capt. Green said, 'that's one of them', and then pointing to Capt. Chambers said, 'that's the other'. The leading man then said to Capt. Green, 'Come on, get out of it' and it was repeated to Capt. Chambers. These two

were stood up and were marched out of the compartment ... after they had left the compartment I put my head out of the window. I saw the two officers marching with their hands up towards the bridge which crosses the railway. On the bridge, which was 50 yards away, I saw a number of civilians and another person with his hands up. The train moved off having been detained for three minutes.[59]

Lieutenant Goode had also been taken off the train but released. The other three officers were then driven to a nearby field where they were shot and buried.[60]

Mick Murphy, commander of the Cork city 2nd Battalion, later placed the Waterfall killings in a wider context. He explained that:

Captain Kelly was in charge of the British intelligence system here and he had six intelligence officers on his staff, and each of them was wiped out one after the other. Three were caught at Waterfall outside the city by some lads from my battalion ... they pulled the three of them off a train on their way to Macroom and shot them.[61]

That same night RIC Sergeant James Donoghue was shot dead by three Volunteers as he was walking down White Street. He had left his home on Tower Street and was heading for Tuckey Street RIC Barracks when figures emerged from the shadows and fired at close range.

With every action by one side now generating a reaction by the other, it was no surprise to anyone that retaliation came quickly.

At around 11.30 p.m., two armed and masked men wearing police uniforms, made their way to the tenement buildings and lane-ways of the area of the city known locally as the 'Marsh'.

At 11.45 p.m. they broke down the door of No. 2 Broad Street and shot Stephen Coleman in the arm as he lay in bed. One of the assailants, armed with a revolver and carrying a flash lamp then rushed upstairs where he found Patrick Hanley standing at the door of his flat, clad only in night-clothes. According to his roommate, John Kenny, Hanley begged not to be shot as he was his mother's chief support, but the man ignored this plea, raised his revolver and fired two shots.[62] The first missed but the second hit Hanley in the chest just above the heart, killing him instantly.

The assailant then entered an adjoining bedroom occupied by the Collins family who were all in bed at the time. He shone his light on the bed and fired a shot that, fortunately for the family, only grazed the head of Mr Collins as he lay alongside his wife and child.

A workshop belonging to a Mr Barry on the ground floor of the building was also broken into but it was not occupied at the time. Having finished with the occupants of this building the two men left but not before lobbing a grenade back through the front door which exploded and wrecked the hall.

The same men then made their way around the corner and broke down the door of No. 17 Broad Lane. Again, one of the men, armed with a revolver and carrying a flash-light, ran up the stairs to where Eugene O'Connell, a twenty-eight-year-old former member of the Munster Fusiliers, lived with his wife and child. When O'Connell came to the door to investigate the noise he was shot in the wrist. As he ran back into his bedroom, his assailant followed him and shot him dead in front of his wife and child.

The assailant then ran up a further flight of stairs towards the flat occupied by the O'Brien family. Mrs O'Brien had already heard the noise and was on her way downstairs. She tried to block the assailant and shouted at him that there was nobody upstairs except her two young sons but she was pushed aside. The man carried on up the stairs and shot her seventeen-year-old son Charles in the mouth, seriously wounding him. The two men then fled the area amidst the screams of the residents. But this night of terror was far from finished.

At four o'clock in the morning, the Coleman family, living at No. 15 North Mall, were awoken by a banging on their front door and a voice shouting 'Military'. James Coleman, the forty-three-year-old proprietor of the Franciscan Well mineral water factory and prominent member of the IDA and Cork Chamber of Commerce got out of bed, threw on some clothes, lit a candle and went to the door. His wife followed close behind, and she later described what happened next:

> When my husband opened the door, a tall man wearing a policeman's cap and heavy overcoat stepped in and asked, 'Are you Coleman?' My husband said 'Yes'. This man then fired two shots point blank at my husband and he fell on the chair beside the door. The man then swung around as if to leave but he again turned and fired two or three shots more.[63]

Coleman had been hit four times, twice in the chest, once in the shoulder and once behind his right ear. While Mrs Coleman and her maid were tending to the dying man an armed Black and Tan came to the door. The maid knew the man and assured Mrs Coleman that he was 'all right'; he in fact offered to go and find a priest and helped place two pillows under Coleman's head before he left.

In retrospect, it is possible to conclude that these killings were far from indiscriminate. The assailants were probably acting on very good information because Charlie O'Brien, his older brother, William, and their neighbour, Justin O'Connor, were all involved in the killing of Sergeant Donoghue. Equally, Patrick Hanley was heavily involved in the republican movement and was a member of Fianna Éireann. However, in the case of James Coleman, the motive may have been somewhat different because following an interview with Mrs Coleman an article later printed in the *Cork Examiner* stated:

> About six or eight weeks ago when the new police came to the barracks there was some trouble about their being supplied with drink in her husband's bar. Two members of the new police visited the bar in a subsequent occasion in search of Mr. Coleman who was not there at the time. One of the men issued a threat at the bar that they would come around at five o'clock next day and shoot Mr. Coleman. The man who said this did call next day, and, brandishing a pistol, fired a shot through the floor. Mr. Coleman was absent, and this same man called on a subsequent occasion, when he again produced a pistol. Mr. Coleman was in his office this time and requested that the man put up the weapon and he would talk to him if he had any grievance to complain of. Mr. Coleman then told him that while he was prepared to serve anybody who conducted himself on the premises he would not be terrorised by threats and had already reported to the military about what happened at his bar.[64]

Throughout the night looters were also active. Roche's Jeweller's on St Patrick's Street was broken into and goods to the value of thousands of pounds were taken. Raiders also broke into the tobacco and chandlery shop belonging to T. O'Callaghan and Sons at 38 North Main Street and removed £150 worth of goods.

News of the night's events soon spread throughout the city and, as the people read the details in the morning's newspapers, the relatives of those who had died prepared to organise the funerals. For the Volunteers of the Cork Brigade none of this served as a deterrent and planning continued apace for their next operation

– the abduction of a senior British army intelligence officer. Danny Healy, the officer commanding the Cork city ASU, later gave the background to the operation:

> Late in the month of November, 1920, we received information from our intelligence service that a senior military intelligence officer would attend mass on a certain Sunday in St Patrick's Church, Lower Glanmire Rd, Cork, accompanied by an intelligence officer from Cork Barracks. We were instructed to kidnap this officer and hand him over to the brigade.[65]

The Volunteers had received information from within Victoria Barracks that the two officers were going to attend the 11.15 a.m. mass on Sunday, 21 November, and so they decided to make their move when the men were leaving the church. That morning, Healy and Seán Culhane, Cornelius O'Sullivan, J. J. O'Connell and Peter Lynch took up positions outside the church. Mass finished around noon and, as the congregation made their way down the steps of the footpath to the road, the Volunteers pulled out their revolvers and detained two men whom they believed to be their targets. However, they had actually captured two RIC constables, Ryan and Carroll, and, having searched both men, Carroll was released but Ryan was bundled into a car and driven away.

News of the abduction reached the RIC barracks at Empress Place within minutes and three lorries of Auxiliaries set off in hot pursuit. As they made their way towards Tivoli the Auxiliaries noticed two men walking on the footpath and opened fire on them seriously wounding Cornelius O'Brien-Corkery. By the time they resumed their search the Volunteers had escaped. Later that night the security forces carried out an extensive search of the city and raided the homes of well known republicans – but they failed to find Ryan.

Shortly after midnight, a bomb was thrown through the front window of the extensive premises of Dwyer and Co. on Washington Street by a number of unidentified men who entered and looted the premises before setting it on fire. The damage to the premises was subsequently estimated to be in the region of £10,000.

It would be another busy night for the members of the fire brigade because three hours after the attack on Dwyer's, the Sinn Féin offices at 56 Grand Parade were also set alight. The RIC later claimed that, 'the building was set on fire by four armed and masked men who are believed to belong to the anti-Sinn Féin League whose personnel and organisation are as secret as those of the Sinn Féin Society.'[66]

But there was still no sign of Ryan and the following notice appeared in Monday's newspapers:

NOTICE

Constable Ryan kidnapped and his comrade robbed while attending Divine Service at St Patrick's Church, Cork, on Sunday, November 21st, 1920.

If Constable Ryan is not returned within 24 hours citizens of Cork beware of the consequences.

(Signed) COMRADES.[67]

The *Cork Examiner* also reported that similar notices stating that unless Ryan was returned there 'would be no peace for the city' and signed 'RIC' were delivered to several Catholic churches in the city. A short time later Ryan was set free when it became clear the Volunteers had the wrong man. Both sides learned some lessons from the affair.

On the British side, it could now be argued that measures undertaken to intimidate the Volunteers by threatening the population actually worked given Ryan's speedy release; in fact, nothing could have been further from the truth. Ryan was released because he was of no value – he had not been the original target – and the Volunteers certainly learned that not all intelligence could be fully relied upon.

However most Volunteer intelligence did prove reliable and that very same Sunday morning a carefully co-ordinated operation was launched by Michael Collins' 'Squad' resulting in the shooting dead of fourteen British intelligence agents.

Retaliation for this was swift. That afternoon a group of Black and Tans and Auxiliaries forced their way into Croke Park as a Gaelic football match between Dublin and Tipperary was being played as a fundraiser for the Irish Volunteers Dependent Fund. One player and fourteen spectators died and over sixty were wounded when the crowd was raked with gunfire. Early the following morning Volunteer officers Dick McKee, Peadar Clancy and Conor Clune were shot dead while being held prisoner in Dublin Castle.

Back in Cork city the war continued unabated and at 2 a.m. the following morning, Tuesday, 23 November, the Sinn Féin Club on Watercourse Road was destroyed by fire. Later that night, shortly before 9 p.m., a bomb explosion occurred at the junction of Princes Street and St Patrick's Street. Volunteers Patrick Trahey, Patrick O'Donoghue and Edward Mehigan were killed and, because a large crowd was walking in the city centre at that time making their way home before curfew, over a dozen people were seriously injured. The explosion also damaged a number of shops in the vicinity, and while there were no uniformed members of the RIC or military in the area at that exact time a motor car had driven up one side of St Patrick's Street, turned around and then passed back by the junction with Princes Street just minutes before the bomb went off.

The identity of the occupants of the car was never discovered but it is reasonable to suggest that they were members of the crown forces.

The Volunteers, however, were also active that night and struck another blow at the British intelligence network when they abducted a former British serviceman and suspected informer named Tom Downing of 8 Castleview Terrace, Lower Road, Cork, as he was on his way to a meeting at the Cork branch of the Federation of Demobilised Sailors and Soldiers.[68]

Before the night was over the Sinn Féin hall situated over the Queenstown Laundry at the bottom of Shandon Street was also destroyed by fire.

A sense of terror had now gripped the people of Cork and it intensified the following day, 24 November, when at 11.40 a.m. a number of Volunteers armed with revolvers robbed the pension offices on South Terrace and got away with £1,000.

That night, at 11 p.m., the Piper's Club on Hardwick Street, which also housed the North-West Ward Sinn Féin Club, was destroyed by fire and at around 5 a.m. the following morning No. 56 Grand Parade was also burned. This three-storey building contained the dental surgery of Mr Goulding, the Artane Clothing Factory Company, the offices of the Irish Assurance Company, the offices of auctioneer Seán Nolan, and a room which was used as a meeting place by members of Sinn Féin.

Later that afternoon, RIC County Inspector Robert Madden was targeted by the Volunteers while walking along the South Mall. A man approached him from behind, pulled out a revolver, and shot him in the head before fleeing down Cook Street. Madden survived the attack and only received a slight wound to his head.

At 9.30 the following morning, 26 November, Cork No. 1 Brigade sustained two further casualties when Volunteers William Mulcahy and Christopher Morrissey were killed by an accidental explosion which ripped through the workshop of undertaker Daniel

O'Leary on Watercourse Road. An hour later, the security forces launched two massive cordon and search operations in the city. One occurred near North and South Main Streets, Washington Street, Grand Parade and Tuckey Street, while the second took place on the Lower Road.

At 2.20 a.m. on, 27 November, a young girl ran into the fire station at Sullivan's Quay and informed the duty officer that No. 53 North Main Street was ablaze. The building housed McGurk's 'Ye Olde Curiosity Shoppe' on the ground floor and offices used by Sinn Féin overhead. Some days earlier an envelope bearing a Cork postmark and addressed to the 'occupiers' of 53 North Main Street had been delivered containing the following note:

FINAL WARNING

You are hereby notified to evacuate the premises herein mentioned, viz. 53 North Main Street, Cork. Ignore this note, and you take the consequences. Policemen and soldiers are being murdered every day, and their barracks blown up without one word of protest from any section in Cork, with the exception of the loyal population.

Signed, B. and T.

God Save the King[69]

There was no one in the building when it was set alight and by the time Captain Hutson and his men arrived, the fire was raging so badly that all they could do was focus on saving the adjoining buildings. Just as Hutson's men started to fight the fire they received a report that smoke was also coming from a tobacconists shop on the corner of Brunswick Street and South Main Street, but when Hutson investigated he discovered the fire was not serious and it was quickly brought under control. However, he fell and injured his hip in the process.

The fire brigade next received news that Douglas Recreational

Hall had been set on fire at around 2.30 a.m. and that a fire had broken out in St Michael's Parochial Hall in Blackrock at 3.15 a.m. – but there was nothing they could do. The brigade simply did not have the resources to deal with this level of arson so they concentrated instead on trying to prevent the flames spreading in North Main Street. But the situation was about to get much worse.

Around 3.30 a.m. two explosions and a number of shots were heard near Cook Street and Oliver Plunkett Street. Thirty minutes later, the fire brigade received reports that a fire was raging in the upper and rear part of the drapery shop owned by Herbert Forrest on St Patrick's Street. Nine people were living on the premises at the time – one male caretaker and eight females who were employed as housekeepers, cooks and servants.

It later emerged that at 2 p.m two armed and masked men had arrived and, having awoken the caretaker by banging on the door, ordered him to evacuate the building. All of the residents, managed to get out before the building was set on fire and were given shelter by a woman who lived over Hipp's shop in Carey's Lane – but Hutson had no way of knowing this at the time as a further series of explosions were heard in the city centre.[70] People living in that area were now completely terrified and most of them gathered what possessions they could carry, believing they would have no choice but to evacuate their homes.

As the end of curfew approached, at 4.45 a.m. a party of masked men in military uniform targeted the home and shop of Sinn Féin alderman, Eamon Coughlan. They forced their way into the premises, and, when they found that the alderman was not there, they ransacked the shop. After they left, his wife, Ellen, discovered that, 'about £20 to £25 worth of cigarettes, about £7 worth of tobacco, and various other things such as cocoa etc were missing'.[71]

As the smoke dissipated and dawn broke it emerged that a notice had been posted around the streets of Cork during the night. It was also printed in the *Cork Examiner* of the day and read as follows:

KIDNAPPING IN CORK
NOTICE
If Mr. Downey *[sic.]* is not returned to his home within 56 hours Cork citizens prepare especially Sinn Féiners.
(signed)
BLACK AND TANS.[72]

That evening, Sinn Féin alderman, Liam de Róiste, commented on Tom Downing's disappearance in his diary: 'I do not exactly know who Mr. Downing is, but he is probably a man that common reports say is in some way attached to the detective force, and the presumption is that he has been captured by some of the Volunteers.'[73] De Róiste was correct. Florrie O'Donoghue had identified Downing as an informer and, completely ignoring the warning posters, he was tried, convicted of spying and executed.[74] The backlash for both the abduction and the attack on Robert Madden was swift in coming.

Shortly after midnight, on the morning of Sunday, 28 November, three buildings on St Patrick's Street were set on fire: Cahill and Co.; Blackthorn House, manufacturers of Irish costumes, umbrellas and walking sticks; and the American Shoe Company. Once again Cork Fire Brigade, now under the command of Acting Superintendent Higgins, because Hutson was on sick leave, was called upon to deal with the conflagration. The brigade had only just begun to fight the fires when a series of loud explosions occurred in all three buildings. These blasts, which were probably caused by exploding petrol canisters, sent the flames high into the night sky. For a while the fires were so intense that it appeared all of the buildings on St Patrick's Street between the junctions of Princes Street and George's Street would be consumed by the flames. As a precaution, all people living in nearby buildings were awoken and evacuated from their homes.

Before 1 a.m. another series of explosions was heard near Camden Quay, and, a short time later, while the firemen were fighting the fires on St Patrick's Street, the fire station on Sullivan's Quay received a report that the Transport and General Workers Union building on the quay was also on fire. A number of firemen were dispatched to deal with this latest blaze and they worked so strenuously that they succeeded in extinguishing the blaze within a half hour. However, at 4 a.m. they received a further report that the building was alight once again and when they attempted to return to the fire, they were prevented from doing so. One fireman later stated to the *Cork Examiner* that:

When we were approaching Patrick's Bridge we saw three or four men turn from the bridge on to Lavitt's Quay and go, as we thought, towards the Opera House. But when we had got thirty yards further and reached the centre of the bridge, they opened fire on us. We halted and one of us shouted to them, 'Don't shoot us anyway'. One of them replied by ordering us to turn back. We obeyed, but just as we had got to Fr Mathew's statue, fire was opened on us from front and rear. One of them shouted to us to turn down a bye-street, and we went down Maylor Street. Why we got this order I don't know, but we went along to Parnell Place across Parnell Bridge and back to our station. We made no further attempt to go to Camden Quay until we were rung up by the city engineer at 7 a.m.[75]

Not surprisingly then, because the fire brigade was prevented from returning to Camden Quay, the Transport and General Workers Union building and some adjoining residential properties were completely destroyed.

Back on St Patrick's Street, the firemen worked bravely throughout the night and, by end of curfew at 5 a.m., all of the fires there had been brought under control. However, both Cahill's and Blackthorn House were destroyed and the premises of the American Shoe Company sustained serious damage. Two other buildings on St Patrick's Street were also attacked that night. The jewellery shop belonging to John Teape had been broken into and a large quantity of merchandise was stolen. Attempts were also made to break into the jewellery shop belonging to Michael Roche but steel shutters inside the door and windows prevented entry. To round off the night's activities four men dressed in civilian attire were observed firing shots into two adjoining garages on South Mall which belonging to J. R. Cross and Messrs Mullins and Sons.

As dawn broke, a second shift of firemen remained on duty in St Patrick's Street hosing down the smouldering buildings. Throughout the day large crowds gathered on the street to witness the devastation. However unknown to all of them a military engagement was about to take place in west Cork which would send shock waves through the British political and military establishments and have a serious knock-on effect in the life of their city.

7

KILMICHAEL

On the morning of Sunday, 28 November, a thirty-six strong Volunteer flying column led by Tom Barry took up ambush positions on both sides of the Macroom to Dunmanway road in the townland of Kilmichael. The intended target was a mobile patrol of Auxiliary cadets from C Company, which was then based in Macroom Castle. The Volunteers waited patiently throughout the day. At around 4 p.m. the first of two lorries carrying the Auxiliaries came into view and Barry, wearing Volunteer tunic, stood out on the road pretending to be a British army officer. Waving to the approaching vehicles he signalled them to slow down and when the first vehicle came near, he hurled a grenade into the cab and started firing. The rest of the column followed suit and in the fire-fight that followed sixteen Auxiliaries were killed. One managed to escape but was subsequently captured and shot dead, and the remaining member was so badly injured that he was thought to be dead and left where he fell. Three Volunteers were killed and two wounded.

These represent the undisputed facts of what happened and they would have a huge impact on both sides as the war continued. However, the disputed facts also had impact – not least amongst which was the question of whether the Auxiliaries in the second lorry deceitfully offered to surrender only to recommence firing, or whether some Auxiliaries genuinely attempted to surrender but Barry ordered all of them to be killed including those already wounded.[76] The reality of the situation is that some reports refer to a false surrender, and others do not. This effectively made it impossible to determine the truth.

However it was without doubt the condition of the bodies when recovered from the scene which generated most reaction on the establishment side. On 29 November, the remains were taken to Macroom Castle where Dr Jeremiah Kelleher examined them. Kelleher's son, Phillip St John Kelleher, had joined the Auxiliaries after a distinguished career in the Leinster Regiment during the war, only to be shot dead at Kiernan's Hotel in Granard, County Longford, on the night of 31 October 1920. When a military court of inquiry was convened at Macroom Castle on 30 November under the chairmanship of Major A. Stapleton of the First Battalion, Manchester Regiment, Dr Kelleher gave the following evidence for the probable cause of death, based on his examination the previous evening; albeit at the time he got some of the names wrong (correct names in italics):

Cadet Hughes *(Hugo)*	Compound fracture of the skull, compound fracture of the thigh bone.
Cadet Lucas	Gunshot wound on head, several wounds on head and body
Cadet Hooper Jones *(Hugh-Jones)*	One wound on back, main arteries cut
Inspector Crake	Gunshot wound in the head.
Captain Graham	Bullet wound on neck
Cadet Pearson	Wound on head, lacerated wound on fore-arm
Cadet Webster	Gaping wound on shoulder, big perforation wound on liver, gunshot fired at close range
Cadet Jones	Wound on back, six other bullet wounds
Cadet Bradshaw	Wound on shoulder, big perforation wound on liver, gunshot fired at close range

Cadet Barnes	Gaping wound on back, four other bullet wounds, gunshot wound over heart inflicted after death.
Cadet Wainwright	Wound over chest and another wound
Cadet Pallister *(Pallester)*	Wound over chest caused by explosive bullet, compound fracture of the skull inflicted by heavy instrument after death
Cadet Taylor	Perforated wound on chest, wound over heart
Cadet Bailey *(Bayley)*	Bullet wound behind the ear and chest
Cadet Gleares *(Gleave)*	Gunshot wound over heart, wound in chest from explosive bullet
Constable Porte *(Poole)*	Bullet wound in chest and shoulder, fracture of bones of face caused by heavy instrument.

While it could be argued that Dr Kelleher was not impartial – given the death of his son at the hands of the Volunteers a month earlier – it must be noted that he was then and remained thereafter a highly respected individual in Macroom – and was never subsequently accused of dishonesty in either the preparation of his report or in the evidence he offered at the inquiry. Either way the conclusions that could be drawn from his evidence indicated that:

1. The Auxiliaries may have been attacked with explosive bullets.
2. Some wounds may have been inflicted after death.
3. Some wounds may have been inflicted at very close range
4. Some wounds could have been inflicted using implements other than firearms.

Kelleher's evidence to the court of inquiry was reported verbatim in the *Cork Constitution* of 1 December 1920. The *Irish Times* followed suit by reporting that 'the bodies have nearly all six bullet wounds, and have suffered terrible mutilation, as though they have been hacked with axes.'[77] The next day, the *Times* of London stated that after the engagement:

> There followed a brutal massacre, the policy of the murder gang being apparently to allow no survivor to disclose their methods. The dead and wounded were hacked about the head with axes, shotguns were fired into their bodies, and they were savagely mutilated. The only survivor, who was wounded, was hit about the head and left for dead. He had also two bullet wounds. The bodies were rifled and even the clothes taken. The ambushing parties departed in lorries. Terrible treachery on the part of the local inhabitants is indicated by the facts that, although many people attending Mass on Sunday morning were diverted from their route by the murder gang, no word was sent to the police, and the ambush sat there until dusk.[78]

These reports had a chilling effect on all members of the crown forces. They indicated, correctly or otherwise, that the Volunteers had descended to a new level of brutality. They also indicated that crown forces were no longer safe even when operating in large convoys, and it painted a graphic picture of the fate which awaited every one of them if defeated.

This was no longer a police campaign – if indeed it had ever been so. It was now beyond any doubt a war where the combatants would have to fight to the death. For those members of the crown forces still trying to cope with chronic post-traumatic stress from their experiences on the Western Front, the pressure now became intense. They could not fight the enemy because they could not see him. They could not see him because he lived behind the cloak of anonymity which was the civilian population. With tension mounting daily behind each barrack wall, it was small wonder that the civilian population was bearing the brunt of these frustrations.

While Barry certainly wished to defeat the Auxiliaries at Kilmichael, it is doubtful if he also wished to inspire them to greater levels of atrocity than before. But that is precisely what happened.

On the other side of the equation, on the afternoon of 29 November, Volunteers from Cork No. 1 Brigade abducted James Blemens from his home on the Blackrock Road. Later, at 7 p.m., they abducted his father, Frederick, an inspector in horticulture and beekeeping with the Department of Agriculture and Technical Instruction for Ireland. Both father and son were believed to be British spies. They were tried by the Volunteers, convicted of being informers, and executed on 2 December.[79]

While it is clear that some people were passing information to the British authorities in Cork at this time, it is by no means proven that an organised spy-ring existed. Neither is it proven that a body calling itself the Anti-Sinn Féin Society ever existed or that large numbers of disaffected Protestants became actively involved in organised attempts to defeat the Volunteers.

A better evaluation would accept that there was Protestant and unionist dissatisfaction with the Volunteers and their methods. Certainly attempts were made to recruit informers and, with money available for this work, there were indeed some applicants. And a black propaganda war was certainly being waged by Captain Kelly and his intelligence staff in Victoria Barracks as they utilised the newspapers to issue threats and notices. With the street-lights turned off by direction of the Corporation, and a curfew in place throughout the night, for those members of the crown forces who wished to engage in reprisals the opportunities were boundless.

Retaliation for the abduction of the Blemens was swift in coming. That night, for the first time since the imposition of curfew, and perhaps in anticipation of large-scale retaliation in the wake of the Kilmichael ambush, the Corporation decided not to extinguish the street-lights in the city. At 11.30 p.m. a loud explosion was heard near Parnell Bridge. One hour later, the fire brigade station on Sullivan's Quay received a report that the Thomas Ashe Sinn Féin Club on Fr Mathew's Quay was on fire. In view of the fact that his men had been shot at while on their way to fight the fire at the Transport and General Worker's Union building, Acting Superintendent Higgins deemed it necessary to obtain a military escort before going to fight this latest outbreak.

A military escort reported to Sullivan's Quay at 1 p.m. and the brigade immediately went to the scene of the fire. By then, the flames were being fanned by strong winds and fire had completely engulfed the building. Higgins decided to concentrate on stopping the fire from spreading but they had no sooner begun than a report was received that City Hall had been set on fire. Leaving a small number of men to deal with the fire in the Sinn Féin Club, Higgins rushed the remainder of the brigade over to City Hall where he found that the public health offices, which had been bombed the previous month, were again on fire. Fortunately, for Higgins the fire was relatively small but when the brigade brought it under control a further report arrived informing him that Egan's Jewellers on St Patrick's Street was also burning. Convinced that the City Hall fire had been extinguished he immediately went to Egan's. He discovered that the rear of the building had been broken into and set on fire but fortunately the fire had not spread and it was quickly extinguished. It was now 3.30 a.m. and the brigade were exhausted but another report was received indicating that City Hall was again on fire! Higgins ordered his men back to City Hall and, together with some of the night watchmen, they managed to extinguish the flames. The night watchmen later reported that a number of armed men had broken into the building and set it on fire and when they tried to extinguish the flames they had been ordered not to do so at the point of a revolver.[80]

By now events in Ireland had come to dominate daily debate in the House of Commons. On 24 November, Sir Hamar Greenwood was challenged over the fact that issue twelve of the RIC *Weekly Summary* carried the notice from the 'Anti-Sinn Féin Society' threatening to shoot members of Sinn Féin. This notice had been printed in the newspapers in Cork the previous October. Lieutenant Commander Kenworthy, the liberal MP for Rotherham, wanted to know who was responsible for placing this notice in an official publication. Joseph Devlin inquired whether Greenwood proposed to 'continue publishing the Summary given that it was in fact paid for by the government, and every copy with this notice in it was an incitement to assassination of civilians in Ireland'.[81]

The chief secretary denied these allegations and informed the House that he intended to continue publishing the *Weekly Summary*. James Hogge then asked if Greenwood would ensure that anything that might be thought to provoke further murders or reprisals was excluded in the future. He replied that he would do what he could to give some personal supervision to the paper but he could not promise to read all the proofs. He then stated that he felt the paper 'served a useful purpose to a sorely tried force'.[82]

Kenworthy returned to the attack on 29 November when he asked the chief secretary if 'he had any information in regard to the alleged burning by forces of the crown of a large shop, a club house and several dwelling houses in the city of Cork on Friday night last [and] whether it was true, as stated, that the police prevented the extinction of the flames at the point of a revolver and whether the burning was still being carried on?' Greenwood acknowledged that the burnings had indeed taken place but stated that the police did not know who had started the fires. He also said that the suggestion that the police had prevented the extinction of the fires was 'without foundation' and they had assisted the fire brigade and prevented lootings.

Kenworthy was unmoved by this reply and he again pressed Greenwood, asking him if he was aware 'that on Saturday several evening papers, including the *London Evening News* said that [the fires] had been done by the Black and Tans [and] if it were not done by them will he have these papers prosecuted.'

Devlin then asked Greenwood if 'it is quite possible to burn a series of buildings, including shops belonging to unionists, in a great city, and he neither knows or seems to care who are the malefactors, nor does he make any attempt to bring them to justice', and if that was his position on the matter.

The chief secretary replied that it was not his position, he had done his best to get answers by telegraph and he was still in the process of making inquiries. Just as the debate concluded, Greenwood received a telegram informing him of events at Kilmichael. Later that night he stood up in the House and read General Tudor's version of events:

The ambush consisted of about 80 to 100 men. All the men in khaki wore steel helmets. The attackers fired from both sides of the road and also directed enfilade fire straight down the road. By force of numbers some of my poor fellows were disarmed and then brutally murdered. Their bodies were rifled. All money and valuables were taken and even articles of clothing were stripped from the corpses.[83]

Notwithstanding this information, the British Labour Party remained determined to investigate the situation in Ireland and the members of their commission departed England on 30 November. While they were on their way the issue of looting burned-out shops began to cause concern to Daniel Cohalan, the Roman Catholic bishop of Cork, who sat down at his office in Farranferris and wrote the following letter, which appeared in the *Cork Examiner* on 1 December:

Dear Sir,

I ask a little of your space to issue a warning against the looting of the establishments which have been ruined by fire.

I know all the temptations which have been put in the way of some of the poor to carry off goods from those establishments, but it is well known that it is not the poor alone who have been guilty.

Now the goods in the ruined houses remain the property of the owners of these establishments. It is sinful to steal or carry off these goods, and persons who have any of these stolen goods in their possession are bound to restore them to their owners.

A considerable amount of property has been returned to the owners. More is yet in concealment. It is known who has have the stolen goods, and I appeal to the people who may have any of the looted property to give it privately to the priests of their parish in order that it may be restored to the owners.

We are passing through a trying crisis, and I appeal to the people to exercise restraint over themselves, to respect the moral law, and to avoid anything that would lead to social disorder in our midst.

Daniel Cohalan
Bishop of Cork

While the bishop was trying to stop the looting, nobody was attempting to stop the arson attacks which had been raging through the city for two weeks and now continued in the early hours of 1 December. Shortly before 4 a.m., a group of five masked men wearing long overcoats and carrying large tins were observed making their way up MacCurtain Street from the direction of Bridge Street. They stopped outside Victoria Buildings which contained Thomas O'Gorman's Gentleman's Outfitters, Dalton's

Restaurant, the offices of the Royal Liver Friendly Society and a number of residential apartments. They broke open the main door and one went inside while the others passed in their tins. Once this was complete, a taper was lit and thrown in through the door. Loud explosions followed and fire broke out on the ground floor. Fortunately, the residents living in the upstairs flats had heard the noise and managed to evacuate the building before the fire spread.

As soon as the fire station at Sullivan's Quay heard of the outbreak they requested a police escort from Union Quay Barracks and then immediately rushed over to MacCurtain Street. As on previous occasions the fire had already spread by the time they arrived. Again, their only option was to try to save the adjoining properties and, while some of these suffered minor damage, the fire was eventually contained and extinguished.

Later that morning the following notice appeared in the *Cork Examiner* and *Cork Constitution*:

ANTI-SINN FÉIN SOCIETY
CORK AND DISTRICT CIRCLE
Membership 2000 and Still Growing
    TO ALL CORK CITIZENS
    TAKE NOTICE that any householders known to shelter any rebel, or who was known to subscribe to any rebel funds, or to assist in any way the murderous gang of assassins known as Sinn Féin, had better increase his or her FIRE AND LIFE INSURANCE, as it will be needed. It will be wiser than buying spurious Dáil Éireann bonds.
REMEMBER 1641.
REMEMBER 1798.
                By Order of the Committee
                        J.P.H.D.[8]

At 1 a.m. on 2 December, the offices of the Irish National Insurance Society on Marlborough Street were destroyed by fire as the British authorities in the city made their final arrangements to pay tribute to the Auxiliaries slain at Kilmichael.

In similar fashion to the manner in which the Volunteers organised the funerals of MacCurtain, MacSwiney and others, the British authorities decided to provide a military and police escort for the remains of the Auxiliaries as they passed through the city streets before being placed on board a ship bound for Britain. On the morning of 2 December the following notice appeared in the morning papers:

NOTICE

The General Officer Commanding 17th Infantry Brigade, Cork, requests that all business premises and shops in Cork be closed between the hours of 11 a.m. and 2 p.m. on Thursday, December 2nd, 1920, as a mark of respect for the Officers, Cadets and Constables of the Auxiliary Company, R.I.C. who were killed in the ambush near KILMICHAEL on the 28th November, 1920, and whose Funeral Procession will be passing through the City on December 2nd.

F. R. Eastwood
Brigade Major, 17th Infantry Brigade

Before the remains of the Auxiliaries left Macroom that morning they were laid into coffins, draped with the Union Jack, and placed on eight Crossley tenders. Two lorries of armed soldiers and two lorries of armed Auxiliaries escorted the remains which were met by large crowds when they arrived at Victoria Cross in Cork city at 11.30 a.m. A bearer party of Auxiliaries and a brass band then joined the procession.

Benjamin Dowse, the Church of Ireland bishop of Cork,

Dean Babbington, Brigadier General Higginson, RIC Divisional Commander Phillip Armstrong Holmes, Colonel Latimer and other religious, military and police dignitaries took their place at the head of the procession which then made its way through the streets to the accompaniment of solemn music. Many shops had closed as requested and the streets were lined with people. On arrival at Custom House Quay the coffins were given a final salute and placed on board the S.S. *Thistle* which then sailed for Britain.

Once the ceremonies were over the mood of the security forces in the city quickly began to change and turned nasty. Civilians going about their business during the day were stopped and searched at random and were often subjected to physical and verbal abuse. While the reputation earned by the Black and Tans in the city was already bad, the Auxiliaries soon surpassed it. Drunkenness and brute force became the hallmarks of Auxiliary operations. Florrie O'Donoghue recorded that since their arrival in Victoria Barracks members of K Company had:

> indulged in raids on houses, holding up and searching civilians in the streets, robbery and insulting behaviour. In November and December their drunken aggressiveness became so pronounced that no person was safe from their molestations. Age or sex was no protection. Poor women were robbed of their few shillings in the streets in broad daylight. After their raids on houses articles of value were frequently missing. Whips were taken from shops with which to flog unoffending pedestrians. Drink was demanded at the point of the revolver.[85]

The *Cork Examiner* provided an account of the terror that gripped the centre of the city on the afternoon of 6 December:

> Small parties of Auxiliary police on foot patrolled the flat of the

city from about three o'clock for some hours and they held up and searched several civilians. There seemed to be no regularity in these searches, for while some people were allowed pass without being questioned or searched, others were held up and thoroughly examined ... The Auxiliaries were holding up and searching people in Patrick's Street, at the corner of Princes Street about 3.45 p.m. and at the same time others were stopping and examining pedestrians on South Mall and Oliver Plunkett Street. Those people who walked with their hands in their pockets came in for particular attention. Almost every man who had his hands in his pockets when seen by the Auxiliaries was ordered to halt and take out his hands. He was then thoroughly searched and his papers etc. closely scrutinised. About four o'clock four or five of the Auxiliaries patrolled up and down St Patrick's Street in a motor-car travelling at a fairly rapid pace. One of the party brandished a revolver and shouted to the people to get off the roadway onto the footpath. From four until five o'clock around Winthrop Street and Oliver Plunkett Street was the principal area of the searches. Several people were held up by the armed Auxiliaries and thoroughly searched. About 4.15 some five or six shots were discharged, apparently by the Auxiliary police in Oliver Plunkett Street near the post office. These shots appear to have been fired in the air, and as far as can be ascertained nobody was injured. A panic however was created when the shots rang out and the crowds that had gathered to watch the proceedings scattered in all directions.[86]

Ironically, on the same day General Tudor actually attempted to bring the police under control when he issued a second memorandum in which he stated:

I wish again to impress on all members of the Police Force the absolute necessity of stopping burnings whatever the provocation. The only justifiable burnings are the destruction of buildings from which fire is opened on Forces of the Crown. Burnings of houses or buildings not directly connected with assassination or attempted assassination, is indefensible.[87]

It was in the midst of this turmoil that the members of the British Labour Commission led by A. G. Cameron, the chairman of the National Executive of the English Labour Party, arrived in Cork to inquire into the situation and conditions in the city. On 6 December, the commission met with the lord mayor, Dónal O'Callaghan, and a number of Sinn Féin councillors who informed them that:

During the month of November alone over 200 curfew arrests had been made, four Sinn Féin clubs burned to the ground, twelve large business premises destroyed by fire, in addition to attempts made to fire others, including the City Hall, seven men shot dead, a dozen men seriously wounded, fifteen trains held up, four publicly placarded threats to the citizens of Cork issued and over 500 houses of private citizens forcibly entered and searched.[88]

The commission remained in the city on 7 December and visited a number of the buildings that had been burned as well as houses and shops where furniture fittings and other properties had been removed during searches. The members also interviewed some witnesses to the attacks that had occurred during the past month. One witness gave the following statement concerning action taken by the Auxiliaries on 6 December:

At between 9 and 9.15 p.m. on December 6, 1920, I had just left my friend [and] I was walking toward my home when I was stopped by some Auxiliary Police. They ordered me to take my hands out of my pockets and hold them up. I did so and one of the Auxiliaries searched me and took everything from my pockets except my watch. The searcher handed the contents of my pockets to the men behind him. They were then handed back to me in one packet and I was told to retrace my steps and go home by another route or I would be shot. When I arrived home I examined my papers and wallet and found that £48 in £1 notes belonging to my firm was missing; also £35 in four £5 notes, one £10 note, and five £1 notes, private money, together with £16 10s 4d, in an envelope being my salary for one month, had disappeared. I have not reported the matter to the police as I fear the consequences.[89]

While the arson attacks stopped during the commission's visit, the conduct of the Auxiliaries did not improve and one witness gave the following description of how the Auxiliaries behaved in the streets of Cork on Tuesday, 7 December:

I was working in Patrick's Street, opposite the Munster Arcade. From 2.30 p.m. to 4.30 p.m. I saw three Auxiliaries, one tall and two small, in khaki uniform and tam-o'-shanter caps, with jarvey whips in their hands and revolvers in their holsters. I saw them continually for the whole two hours beating indiscriminately every male that came within reach of their whips, as they walked to and fro between Patrick's Bridge and where I was working. I saw one of them whipping a middle-aged man, from Morgan Street to Victoria Hotel, a distance of about 100 yards. The man turned around on the Auxiliary and protested, but the answer to this was, 'Get on, you Irish swine', repeating it several times. I dodged them on several occasions and escaped. During the two hours that this continued, the patience and restraint of the people was wonderful under such humiliating provocation; women and children fled panic-stricken and terrified with every rush the Auxiliaries made.[90]

That same afternoon, at around 4.35 p.m., a number of local men were walking down the Lower Road near the corner of Winter Street when they met two lorries travelling in the direction of the city. A number of shots were fired from these lorries and one of the men, John Fleming of 17 Cattle Market Avenue, was shot in the abdomen. He was rushed to the North Infirmary Hospital but died on the operating table at around 8 p.m.

The members of the Labour Commission left Cork for Tralee on the morning of 8 December but there was no let-up in either military or police activity. Then at 9.10 p.m. a young man, Francis Murphy from 18 Tower Street, was shot dead outside SS Peter and Paul's church. The annual triduum of the Young Men's Society was due to have opened in the church at 8 p.m. but because of the ongoing situation in the city it was deferred. Instead, the rosary was said, followed by a short sermon by Fr J. C. O'Flynn, a curate from the North Cathedral. As the congregation was leaving the church a number of shots rang out from the direction of St Patrick's Street. In addition to killing Murphy, a number of other people were wounded and taken to hospital for treatment.

The next day, Thursday, 9 December, a group of armed Volunteers forced their way into the home of George Horgan at Mathew Place, Ballintemple, and abducted him.[91] The Volunteers believed Horgan was a spy and tried and convicted him before carrying out his execution three days later.[92] He was buried in a shallow grave in a wooded area at Lakelands, off Crawford's Road, Blackrock.[93] They appeared to have correctly identified Horgan as a spy because the following notice appeared in the *Cork Examiner* on 10 December:

NOTICE

IF G. Horgan is not returned by 4 o'clock on Today (Friday),
10th December, Rebels of Cork, Beware, as one man and one shop
shall disappear for each hour after the given time.

(Signed)

'B's and T's.'[94]

The same paper also carried another warning:

IMPORTANT NOTICE

We, the undersigned, do now give the male sex of Cork city
notice, 'which must be adhered to forthwith', that any persons of
the said sex who is seen or found loitering on street corners or on
the pathways without reasonable excuse why he should be there, or
any man or boy found to be standing or walking with one or both
hands in his pockets will, if he does not adhere to this order, suffer
the consequences which will no doubt ensue.

(Signed)

Secretary of Death or Victory League.

God Save The King

and

Frustrate His Enemies

Also that morning, at around 6 a.m., an elderly man named
Andrew Forbes from College Road who was in the city to collect
the daily newspapers before going to work, was shot in the foot
at the corner of Marlborough Street and St Patrick's Street. Fortunately, the wound was not serious and Forbes later claimed that
the shot that hit him came from Hipp's Outfitter's shop on St
Patrick's Street which was being looted at the time.[95]

However, the most significant development that Friday was
the introduction of Martial Law in the southern part of Ireland.
The text of the proclamation issued by lord lieutenant of Ireland,

Field Marshal French, was as follows:

MARTIAL LAW PROCLAMATION

Whereas certain evilly disposed persons and associations, with the intent to subvert the supremacy of the Crown in Ireland, have committed divers acts of violence, whereby many persons, including members of the forces of the Crown and other servants of his Majesty have been murdered, and many others have suffered grievous injuries and much destruction of property has been caused.

And whereas in certain parts of Ireland disaffection and unrest have been especially prevalent, and repeated murderous attacks have been made upon members of his Majesty's forces, culminating in the ambush, massacre and mutilation with axes of 16 cadets of the Auxiliary Division, all of whom had served in the late war, by a body of men who were wearing trench helmets and were disguised in the uniforms of British soldiers, and who are still at large.

Now I, John Denton Pinkstown Viscount French, Lord Lieutenant General and General Governor of Ireland, do hereby proclaim by virtue of all the powers thereunto enabling that the following counties, namely:

- The county of Cork, East Riding and West Riding.
- The county of Tipperary, North Riding.
- The county of Tipperary, South Riding.
- The county of Kerry.
- The county of Limerick.
- The county of the city of Limerick.

Are, and until further Order, shall continue to be under and subject to Martial Law.

And I do hereby call on all loyal and well-affected subjects of the Crown to aid in upholding and maintaining the peace of this Realm, and the supremacy and authority of the Crown, and to obey and confirm all Orders and Regulations of the military authorities issued by virtue of this proclamation.

Given at his Majesty's Castle of Dublin this 10th day of December, 1920.

FRENCH.

God Save the King.[96]

Taken in the context of the repression already being administered by the security forces, this additional measure was both an admission that the situation was out of control and a very severe response. Under the provisions of Martial Law:

- All meetings of six or more persons in a public place were banned.
- All householders and hoteliers were obliged to affix a list to the inside of the main door of their establishment that showed the name, age, sex and occupation of all those who resided therein.
- Any unauthorised person found to be in possession of arms, ammunition or explosives would, on conviction by military court, be liable to suffer death.
- Any unauthorised person wearing the uniform or equipment of British forces or similar clothing likely to deceive would, on conviction by military court, be liable to suffer death.
- Any person taking part in, or aiding or abetting those taking part in insurrection would be considered guilty of waging war against the king and would, on conviction by military court, be liable to suffer death.[97]

But neither the introduction of Martial Law nor the ongoing warnings published in the press had any influence on the Volunteers of Cork No. 1 Brigade. As far as they were concerned, the situation had long passed the point of no return and although this was not an even contest, and the odds were stacked against them, the Volunteers were now determined that the conduct and activities of the Auxiliaries in K Company would not go unchallenged.

8

DILLON'S CROSS

Outraged by the deaths of their comrades at Kilmichael, enraged at the details of Dr Kelleher's post mortem examination, frustrated that they could not fight their enemy in a conventional way, and already enduring post traumatic stress from their individual wartime experiences, the Auxiliaries of K Company continued to vent their anger upon the ordinary citizens of Cork. However, they were faced by Volunteers determined to build on the momentum of Tom Barry's success, and early in December Seán O'Hegarty ordered all Volunteer units to launch attacks on the Auxiliaries as soon as possible.

It soon emerged that a mobile patrol comprising two lorries usually left Victoria Barracks around 8 o'clock each night and made its way towards the city centre via the Old Youghal Road and Dillon's Cross. To achieve the element of surprise it was decided to mount an ambush on the patrol as close to the barracks as possible thereby hitting the Auxiliaries at a time and place where they would be most vulnerable and where they would least expect it.

The previous year, Volunteer James O'Mahony from the 1st Battalion had carried out a detailed reconnaissance of the locality to select potential ambush sites. The site selected which gave the Volunteers best advantage was as an old stone wall which ran for forty metres between Balmoral Terrace on the north side of the Old Youghal Road and the shop and houses on the corner of

Dillon's Cross. Behind this wall was an open area, known locally as O'Callaghan's field, which led down into the Glen and would provide an excellent escape route if and when the time came.

But the proximity of the proposed ambush site to Victoria Barracks (300 yards) also posed problems. Once it became clear that an attack was underway, reinforcements could be deployed to the scene within minutes. Therefore any offensive action by the Volunteers would have to be short and sharp; simplicity would be the key to success. The plan involved stopping the Auxiliary patrol, hurling grenades into the lorries, firing a quick volley from revolvers, and then disappearing as quickly as possible by melting back into the civilian population.

The operation began on the night of 8 December. A unit of fifteen Volunteers, commanded by Captain Seán O'Donoghue, and with Riobárd Langford as second-in-command, armed themselves with revolvers and twelve hand grenades and took up position behind the stone wall. A scout was posted further up the road near the barracks and once the Auxiliary patrol had been identified, his task was to alert the others now hunkered down behind the wall by blowing on a whistle. Seán Healy was a member of the unit and later recalled:

> we heard numerous lorries of military passing to and fro, but the Auxiliaries made no appearance that night. They probably went in the opposite direction, as the city could also be reached by another route. After what appeared to be an interminable hour of waiting and watching, we had to disperse, in order to reach home before curfew hour, which was 10 p.m. At least 1,000 troops would pour out of the Victoria Barracks at this hour and take over complete control of the city.[98]

Each man took his revolver home with him that night but the

grenades were collected by Anne Barry of Cumann na mBan and stored close by at her home at No. 8 Windsor Cottages on the Ballyhooley Road. This was an act of exceptional bravery given the ongoing risk of discovery and especially since word of the planned ambush had apparently leaked to the ears of the authorities in Victoria Barracks. A large loyalist population lived in the area of Dillon's Cross at that time and included many women married or related to serving members of the RIC and British army. For these people, Volunteer activity in their area was completely unacceptable, so the presence of the ambush party was reported and a strong military force saturated the area on the following two nights.

However, at around 4 p.m. on Saturday, 11 December, Seán O'Donoghue received information that a patrol consisting of two lorries of Auxiliaries would again leave Victoria Barracks that night and travelling with them this time would be the key British intelligence officer, Captain James Kelly. O'Donoghue decided to seize this opportunity but given such short notice he was only able to muster five local men: – Seán Healy, Michael Baylor, James O'Mahony, Augustine O'Leary, and Michael Kenny. He had two objectives: first, to inflict maximum damage on the Auxiliary patrol; and second, as Michael Kenny later stated – to capture or kill Captain Kelly.[99]

As darkness fell that Saturday evening O'Donoghue's men made their way back to Dillon's Cross. Anne Barry was also on the move quietly transferring the grenades from her own house and hiding them in the front garden of a house owned by the Lennox family at 'Mount View', Ballyhooley Road. At around 6.30 p.m. James O'Mahony collected the grenades and distributed them between the ambush party as they arrived to take their positions.

Michael Kenny was nominated to act as the scout in the hope that he might also be able to positively identify Captain Kelly.

He took up position openly on the road at Harrington Square while the remainder again took cover behind the stone wall in O'Callaghan's field across the road. The tactics adopted by O'Donoghue were virtually the same as those employed by Tom Barry at Kilmichael. Kenny was dressed in a macintosh overcoat, scarf and cap, in an effort to resemble an off-duty British officer and when the lorries approached his task was to make a hand signal which would encourage the driver of the lead vehicle to either slow down or stop. Then he would make two sharp whistle blasts and the Volunteers behind the wall would engage the enemy.

At around 8 p.m. two Crossley tenders each carrying thirteen Auxiliaries emerged from Victoria Barracks and moved off down the hill towards Dillon's Cross. As the lead vehicle approached, Kenny raised his hand and the patrol slowed down as it passed him. Two shrill whistle blasts rang through the night air and O'Donoghue gave the order to open fire. The ambush party then stood up and Michael Baylor and Augustine O'Leary each threw a grenade at the first lorry while O'Donoghue, Seán Healy and James O'Mahony, targeted the second. Cadet John Leslie Emanuel who was travelling in the first lorry later recalled that the first grenade landed in his lap and although he managed to throw it out a second grenade landed amongst them and blew them all out of the lorry.[100]

As the grenades detonated, the Volunteers drew their revolvers and fired a volley of shots at the patrol before quickly making their escape towards the Glen.

One resident of Dillon's Cross had just been sitting down to tea with his family and he later recalled:

Suddenly we were all brought to our feet by the sound of a grenade exploding somewhere outside followed soon afterwards by two further explosions. Then, after a silence there was shouting and a shot from a revolver, and rifle shots being fired outside. I ran upstairs to the bedroom window and by the light of the gas lamp across the way and a public house I saw a scattered body of Auxiliaries racing down the road, shouting and shooting for all they were worth. This went on for quite a while until somebody took charge of them and got them into some sort of order and started a house to house search.[101]

Confused, disoriented and wounded the Auxiliaries stumbled from their lorries and tried as best they could to extract themselves from the killing zone. Some managed to fire their rifles in the direction of the Volunteers while others dragged the wounded to the nearest cover – in this case O'Sullivan's public house at Dillon's Cross. Here the Auxiliaries charged into the premises with weapons drawn and ordered all customers to put their hands over their heads to be searched. The proprietor, Nora O'Sullivan, immediately tried to calm the situation by telling the Auxiliaries that they had nothing to fear because all her customers were loyal ex-servicemen but this had precisely the opposite effect. In a direct reference to Tom Barry, one of them screamed at her that, 'it was an ex-serviceman who killed all our men at Kilmichael'.

The Auxiliaries then ordered Mary O'Connell, the proprietor's nineteen- year-old niece, and Michael Kenny's girlfriend, to attend the injured and dress their wounds. In their haste they failed to conduct a proper search of the premises but had they done so they would have discovered that, before the ambush, Kenny had asked O'Connell to store a small cache of weapons and ammunition in an upstairs bedroom. As she tended the wounded O'Connell silently prayed that the cache would not be discovered and fortunately her prayers were answered.

By now, the sound of explosions and gunfire had been heard in Victoria Barracks and reinforcements and an ambulance were immediately dispatched to Dillon's Cross. Searchlights were also brought out to illuminate the area from O'Callaghan's field down to the Glen and a search party, accompanied by a pack of bloodhounds, set off in pursuit of the ambush party.

While this was happening Mary O'Connell was standing at the front door of the public house. She witnessed a number of young men being rounded up and forced to lie on the ground at the entrance to St Mary's Avenue. One of them was then dragged to the centre of the crossroads, stripped naked, whipped repeatedly and forced to sing 'God Save the King' until he collapsed on the road.

By this time, O'Donoghue and his men had escaped having run through the Glen into the open countryside outside Blackpool from where they dispersed. Seán Healy went to the railway tunnel which runs beneath Victoria Barracks and stashed his weapon. He later recalled that:

> it was now a case of every man for himself to try and make a safe getaway. Under cover of darkness, and hugging the walls, we ran towards Goulding's Glen and reached it in safety. A large stream ran through the Glen. This was swollen by the winter rains. We crossed the bridge over the stream and got away into the open country near Blackpool. I stayed at the house of Lieut. D. Duggan's father on that eventful night. Bloodhounds were used in the search, but all their efforts to trace us failed.[102]

Michael Baylor and Augustine O'Leary headed off towards the city. Seán O'Donoghue and James O'Mahony made their way to the Delany farm at Dublin Hill. O'Donoghue was still carrying some unused grenades and these were hidden on the Delany farm after which the two men split up and went their separate ways.[103] By now Kenny had also disappeared from the scene. He had run between the houses at the top of Harrington Square, then down Ballyhooley Road and up Gardiner's Hill, before eventually making his way to a Volunteer 'safe-house' at Rathcooney.

The official British account of the Dillon's Cross ambush, later issued by the war office in London, read as follows:

> twelve cadets were wounded, and one has since died of his wounds. Bombs are believed to have been thrown from houses at Dillon's Cross, in the north district of Cork, into lorries containing cadets as they were leaving Cork military barracks. It is suggested that the bombs used were supplied to the assailants from the bomb factory which was discovered in Dublin, and in connection with which four men have been arrested. The ambush took place at 8 p.m. So far as can be ascertained, the attackers of the ambushed cadets escaped.[104]

From the Volunteers' perspective the Dillon's Cross ambush was a spectacular success notwithstanding that Captain Kelly was neither eliminated nor captured. It clearly demonstrated to the Auxiliaries, and to the military authorities in Victoria Barracks, that safety could not be guaranteed anywhere and patrols were vulnerable just 300 yards from where they were garrisoned. But the euphoria of success was short lived as the city braced itself for the predictable reprisal. However no one could possibly have foreseen what lay ahead as the Volunteer victory was about to be transformed into a night of unprecedented terror and arson.

9

REVENGE

Incensed by an attack in such close proximity to their headquarters, and still seeking retribution for the deaths of their colleagues at Kilmichael, the Auxiliaries in Victoria Barracks assembled to exact their revenge. Their response would be swift and devastating and send a clear message to the citizens of Cork that violence against the crown forces in Ireland had a very high price attached to it.

At approximately 9.30 p.m. lorries laden down with armed Auxiliaries and British soldiers left the barracks for Dillon's Cross where they dismounted, made their way to a number of houses, broke open the doors, and forced the occupants on to the street. Once vacant the Auxiliaries then proceeded to set the houses alight; among those targeted was the former home of Brian Dillon, the famous Cork Fenian after whom the cross-roads was named. They then stood guard as several houses were razed to the ground and when some poor unfortunates tried to intervene to save their homes, they were fired upon.

One resident of Dillon's Cross, who struggled to save his own home from burning to the ground later described what happened that night:

While in the act of saving my own home from the encroaching flames, two members of the Crown forces, dressed in khaki uniforms, tam-o'-shanter caps and carrying revolvers in hand, jumped on me, roaring and demanding to know what I was doing. I replied, 'saving our furniture'. They asked, 'were you in the war?' I said, 'No' and immediately I was dealt a severe blow on the face by one of them, causing my teeth to come through my upper lip. I was then dragged into a neighbour's backyard, placed up against a wall there by the taller of them. What happened there I can't remember, but one of my sisters pleaded for my life, and the answer she got was that his heart was as hard as the wall and that it was no use speaking.

From here I was taken out to Dillon's Cross, and while here I was surrounded by Crown forces dressed in khaki and tasselled caps. They carried revolvers and made use of terrible language. They were accompanied by a civilian of low stature; fresh, fair features; wearing a light overcoat and black tweed hat. His language was more frightful that his companions. He spoke with a foreign accent and asked me to point out the houses of Sinn Féiners. This I said I could not do. I was also asked questions about an ambush by another of them, but told him that I knew nothing about it. Then when I was preparing for the worst, on account of their threatening demeanour, a soldier, a private in the Hants. Regiment, rushed on me. He saved my life, and managed to get me near my own house. Here I was again met by one of the Crown forces, who questioned me and asked me to sing 'God save the King' but the good soldier stood by me and managed to get me safe in home.

An Auxiliary, who was standing by the door, followed us into the kitchen. He was a fine big man, dressed in R.I.C. frieze overcoat, soldier's ordinary military cap, and khaki trousers. He was a walking arsenal, his pockets bulging out with bombs. These he showed us and offered to make us a present of them. He said he was an Auxiliary, and they, the Auxiliaries, were going to blow up the city. He said he was due to go at 1 a.m. He left shortly after midnight ... While I was at Dillon's Cross under threats of being shot, I saw an ordinary 'Tommy' bring a small bath full of paraffin or petrol, probably the former, from some house nearby, and throw the contents onto Brian Dillon's house which was burning rapidly. Auxiliaries were looking on at this. A red cross ambulance, military, was stationed nearby on my left.

While indoors with my father, brothers, and sisters, we went through a terrible time. The house next door was by this time fiercely burning, and the fire was gradually encroaching on ours, but we dared not move to save either. The Crown forces kept guard over the burning houses, and anybody trying to save even their own property was fired on.[105]

While the Auxiliaries were busy wreaking havoc at Dillon's Cross, four drivers who had earlier conveyed the members of the British Labour Party Commission to the railway station at Limerick Junction drove into the area. The cars were stopped and the drivers were dragged out and placed up against the wall by the Auxiliaries who refused to listen to their explanations or examine their special permits. Instead, they threatened to shoot the terrified men but were forbidden to do so by an officer who intervened and said the men could not be shot until they were taken to the barracks to be searched. They were then marched up to Victoria Barracks, searched and flung into a small cell in the guardroom which was already occupied by seven other men.[106]

In the meantime, parishioners who had been attending confession in the nearby St Joseph's church heard the sound of the ambush and rushed from the church to the safety of their homes. Some who were living nearby managed to reach home safely while others who normally went home by way of Dillon's Cross had an altogether different experience:

I came out of the church and I saw, looking down from the hill into the hollow at Dillon's Cross I saw the flames from some house that

were burning and I heard some shots being fired. So I went from
there to a friend's house and there happened to be there another
lady from the same terrace and we decided that since she had only
her mother at home that we would make an effort to get home. So
the only way we could get home was to bypass Dillon's Cross and
go down Gardiner's Hill to St Luke's and go up Cassidy's Avenue
to the Old Youghal Road. We went down the Old Youghal Road
past several Black and Tans with petrol tins that took no notice of
us ... The young lady happened to live in the middle of the terrace
so I went down to see her in the gate and as I turned from the gate,
from the shadow of a big long wall opposite ... four or five Black
and Tans came over and a voice said, 'search that man and watch
the house tops'.[107]

In all six houses were burned at Dillon's Cross. The first building
set on fire was Buttimer's Shop at the corner of St Mary's Avenue
but when it was established that the Buttimers were a Protestant
family the fire was quickly extinguished. The second house
attacked was No. 251 Old Youghal Road, which quickly burned
to the ground. Brian Dillon House was the next target. It housed
a butcher's shop run by the O'Hare family and was attacked by
several Auxiliaries. As the building became engulfed in flames the
smell of burning meat pervaded the entire area. No. 10 St Bridget's
Villas was the fourth house set alight. This was the home of a well
known Volunteer, William Sheehan, and was unoccupied at the
time of its destruction. The fifth house to be burned was across the
road from St Bridget's Villas and the the last house set on fire was
at Harrington's Row.

By now word of the ambush had spread to the city centre where
those still out and about were rushing to get home before curfew
hour at 10 p.m. A priest who had been on duty in SS Peter and
Paul's church that evening, and who had succeeded in getting on

the last north-bound tram to leave Fr Mathew's statue at 9 p.m. later recalled the horrific fate suffered by the passengers:

> As the tram passed through MacCurtain Street signs of confusion were visible in the streets outside … Just as the tram was about to ascend Summerhill a lorry full of armed men dashed past us shouting and jeering as they went up the hill. The tram proceeded on its way up the hill to a distance of about 100 yards beyond the RIC barracks, at Empress Place … when suddenly two men (well dressed and with distinct English accents) dashed out into our tram, and at the point of the revolver drove all inside, with me, out. A rush was made for the door at the driver's end of the car and as that side was soon blocked I, being in the middle, could not of course, move till the others had crushed their way out. However the gentlemen with the revolvers insisted that I should, and so they kept knocking me in the side, on my face, and around the head with their revolvers. Repeatedly I told them that I would go as soon as the door was clear, at the same time asking them what was the meaning of treating me like that. As soon as the way was clear I did make towards the door but on my way was forcibly pushed from behind, fell forward, tripped over something on the landing stage of the car, and was pitched out on my face and hands in the middle of the road.
>
> Even in my fall I could see that the tram had been surrounded by armed men, and on getting to my feet I counted about a dozen or more men dressed in long black coats like rain coats, with khaki coloured bands or straps over their shoulders and cross-wires in front, and wearing black tam-o'-shanter caps; each of these uniformed men was armed with a rifle. Immediately I recognised them as forces of the Crown. As soon as I got to my feet I found myself in a scene of great confusion; the uniformed forces of the Crown were rushing at men and women indiscriminately, shouting and beating us with the butts of their rifles and firing in all directions; the 'gentlemen' with

the revolvers were raging all around the tram with much cursing and blasphemy, and were issuing orders to the uniformed forces of the Crown. Three or four women I saw beaten by the 'gentlemen' in mufti ... One woman was knocked to the ground and kicked by a uniformed man as she lay there helpless and screaming. I made a move to assist this poor woman when one of the 'gentlemen' with the English accent roared out that if any man stirred he would be shot there and then. I tried to remonstrate, but my voice was absolutely lost in the general confusion.

All of the men were now ordered to the wall on either side of the ambushed tram, and were roughly told by the 'gentlemen' with the revolvers to 'put up our hands'. Then one of the uniformed men, apparently to make sure that we had our backs to the wall, prodded each one of us with the muzzle of his rifle. Then the 'gentlemen' in mufti came before each man threatening us again with their revolvers, and searching and kicking and shouting that they were going to revenge themselves on us and on the city for what had happened on the hill that night. . The 'gentleman' who had me in hand discovered on tearing open my coat that I was a priest, and he became very excited, shouting that he had got one of the bloody fellows who advised the people to shoot them ... Tearing open my inside coat and my vest he continued to search all my pockets, removing anything I had, including my watch and some money (about 80 shillings). These he kept for himself, and whatever papers and books (including my breviary) he found he kicked out onto the road.

Meantime the other men were being searched and abused, and the tram was being smashed by the men in black uniforms. According as the search of each man was completed he was pushed and kicked and then told he could go. But I being a priest was held over till all had been searched, they were going to revenge themselves on me and on the town that night, so they kept saying. They all now gathered round me shouting and cursing the pope, the bishop, and all the Catholic clergy in general. One of them rushed on me, tore off my overcoat, my inside coat, vest and collar, and pushed me up against the wall, saying that I was to be shot. All retired to the middle of the road, and I began to feel that my end had surely come. In the half light of the place I could not see very well, but they appeared to be debating with one another about me. Suddenly one of the 'gentleman' with the revolver rushed over and roared at me to kneel down, but before I had time to do so he flung me sprawling to the ground. He said that if I write or say 'To hell with the Pope', I would be let off. I said that surely they would not expect a Catholic priest to say this.

At this point some of the 'gentlemen' in the middle of the road shouted to 'let that bastard go', and the 'gentleman' who had me on the ground kicked me and told me to clear off. I got up as well and as quickly as I could, and as I was about to go I was kicked again and told I should run. Being scarcely able to walk from all the bruises and kicks I had received, I was quite unable to carry out the latter command. One of the uniformed men ran at me with his rifle, saying he would make me run, and began to push me violently in the back with the muzzle of his rifle. Thus pushed from behind I stumbled forward up the hill for about twenty yards or so. Then I was suddenly grabbed by the shirt collar, and kicked severely and told if I turned around I would be shot. Without looking round I asked him for my clothes, but I found they had been kicked up the hill a few feet before me. I was putting them on as hastily as I could when a shot rang out in my direction. Fortunately, I was not hit and I hobbled home as best I could.[108]

Further down Summerhill, a group of Black and Tans gathered at the Soldier's Home on MacCurtain Street and began causing mayhem. A pedestrian walking towards the Great Southern and

Western Railway station on the Lower Glanmire Road described what happened:

> The whole party of them, numbering from fourteen and eighteen, opened fire without the slightest warning or provocation. The firing was indiscriminate, going in all directions. Bullets were hopping and whizzing everywhere. Girls, women and children were in a fainting condition, crouching in doorways and running helter skelter for shelter. The corner of MacCurtain Street was like 'hell let loose' with the firing and roaring. The streets became deserted in a few minutes. I took early refuge in the station, and could hear the rifle firing and revolver firing continuing for upwards of twenty minutes. The station was soon filled with panic stricken people who from their own relatings had undergone terrible experiences.[109]

A university student who was making his way home about 9.25 p.m. was held up by a group of five armed men in RIC uniform at the corner of Coburg Street and St Patrick's Hill:

> One of them ordered me to put up my hands. This I did. They then forced me backwards till my back was to the wall, and they told me they were going to shoot me. They kept me in that position for five or ten minutes. Now and then one of them put a barrel of a revolver to my face and lifted it upwards, hitting my nose, and told me to keep my head back. I was then asked to say 'God Save the King', one of them informing me first I would be shot this way or that. I refused. Most of the men were drunk. One less drunk than the others said to give me a chance. Turning to me he said, 'Run up that _____ hill and we'll fire after you'. I ran up the hill [St Patrick's Hill], and they fired after me. I was not hit.[110]

By now the terror had spread to St Patrick's Street. One resident living in a flat overlooking the street heard the sounds of shouting and shots outside his window at 8.55 p.m.:

> I looked out through my window … and saw a Crossley car filled with men, two of whom I could see: they were Auxiliaries with tasselled caps. The shouting and commotion led me to believe that they were holding up citizens on the bridge. The lorry drove away and I saw seven or nine men dressed in civilian clothes come from the bridge and proceed along Patrick's Street. They halted three other civilians at Evans' (bookseller, Patrick's Street), seemingly questioning them as to their identity. I saw one of the seven civilians go over to Evans' window and deliberately smash it with something heavy which he held in his hand. During this time the three civilians were allowed to proceed on their way, and one of the seven civilians was shouting to the others on the bridge 'Come on'. I thought the accent was an Irish one. Three more civilians joined them in response, and firing indiscriminately around the street they disappeared along Patrick's Street in the direction of mid-Patrick's Street. The street was empty of all people at this time.[111]

Foreign visitors to the city were not immune from harassment either. Emil Pezolt, an American sailor on the U.S.S. *West Cannon* which was berthed in Cork at the time, was staying in the Victoria Hotel. Around 9.30 he was making his way back to the hotel when he was held up by a number of Black and Tans who beat him and robbed him of his watch, about $30 in money, and his seaman's passport.[112]

At about the same time, the final curtain came down on the last act of *The Gondoliers* which was playing in the Opera House. On leaving the building, the patrons quickly became aware that something was wrong in the city. Among those who saw *The Gondoliers* that night was Geraldine Sullivan, a member of

Cumann na mBan, her younger sister, Una, and her fiancé, Seán Neeson – an intelligence officer in the Irish Volunteers. She later wrote about what occurred when the play ended:

> We had left the Opera House as planned and turned along the quay towards St Patrick's Street when Seán noticed that something was wrong and turned us back. He had seen a burning tram. Almost immediately we could hear the shouting and smell the burning. We walked home to Sunday's Well, across the North Gate Bridge and along the North Mall. Seán left us at the North Gate Bridge to try and get under cover as quickly as possible as he was in danger of being stopped and recognised.[113]

Another patron of the Opera House wasn't able to get home that night and took shelter elsewhere:

> I was with a friend who was playing 'Giuseppe' (Jack Holland) … and we decided that as we had to go to the south side of the city that it would be wiser not to attempt to go through Patrick's Street so we went up the quay up to Cornmarket Street and cut through Cornmarket Street to the Queen's Old Castle. Before we arrived there actually there was firing and a lot of bustle and excitement there so we got a bit scared and we winded our way back to the Coal Quay where we found a friendly house where we knew we would be welcome – and the chance of getting a drink. We stayed there of course and watched out where there was a lot of movement in the Bridewell, Black and Tans rushing here and there.[114]

But, the worst was yet to come. The tram that had been set on fire near Fr Mathew's statue was but the first of many fires that would be lit in the city centre that night. Alan J. Ellis, a young reporter with the *Cork Examiner* was visiting his cousin, Mickey Hussey, in his rooms at Cornmarket Street and throughout the evening both men heard the sounds of sporadic gunfire. Hussey, concerned for his cousin's safety, urged Ellis to return home before the onset of curfew. Ellis was then living on the northern part of Sunday's Well Road and he wasn't unduly worried about walking the city streets after dark. By that time he had grown quite used to the sounds of gunfire and, just that afternoon, he had in any case been issued with a special pass signed by General Strickland which stated that he was a journalist and allowed to travel during curfew.

When he eventually left his cousin's flat around 9. 30 p.m. the last tram for the north side of the city had already departed from Fr Matthew's statue at 9 p.m. so he decided to call into the *Cork Examiner* offices on St Patrick's Street where he hoped to get a lift from one of the night staff who owned a motorcycle. Ellis later recalled what happened when he turned onto St Patrick's Street from Castle Street:

I soon became aware that something unusual was happening. There had been sporadic gunfire all evening and my ears had grown so accustomed to it that I did not really notice it. I then became aware of the thud of explosions. I knew by then what a bomb sounded like. There were numerous groups of Auxiliaries ... as vicious a bunch of thugs as ever I would encounter. There were also regular soldiers about. I could hear sporadic rifle fire and small arms from every direction.

At first I thought it was an engagement between republicans and the military. Then I noticed, further down Patrick's Street, the 'Auxies' and soldiers were driving people from the streets and firing over their heads to make them disperse into the buildings. Grant's drapery store appeared to be on fire but there was a small unit of the fire brigade on hand. I spoke to a fireman who told me that there had been an ambush at Dillon's Cross ... and there were some dead and injured … Some house had been set on fire in Dillon's Cross and someone had called the fire brigade's Grattan Street depot. The crew were heading for Dillon's Cross, taking the route along Patrick's Street, over the bridge, but then they saw the fire at Grant's store and stopped to deal with it. However, a messenger had been sent to get more fire appliances from the fire brigade headquarters at Sullivan's Quay, which was not far away. I was then joined by a man who swore that earlier he had seen a patrol of Auxiliaries marching up the street with an officer at their head. He said that they had halted in disciplined fashion and on a word of command had broken into Grant's and set it ablaze. My informant said one of them noticed him and came across, shoving a gun into his face and had told him to leave or else! He said that he had hid himself in a nearby building, as he knew what the Auxiliaries were like. More of them appeared and they then moved down the street. He had only re-emerged when he saw the firemen arrive.

Now I realised that all the principal buildings along Patrick's Street had suddenly burst into flames. There is no doubt who was causing the fires. At Munster Arcade, a residential block, the British military ordered people out at gunpoint, shots were fired at the windows and incendiary bombs were thrown in. Some attackers, while not hiding their uniforms, wore scarves over their faces.[115]

Patrick Barry was employed as a dispatch clerk in the Munster Arcade and he also had quarters in the domestic part of the building together with two apprentices and three female members of staff. On that Saturday night he locked up the domestic part of the premises about 9.30 p.m. Some time later he was in his apartment when the housekeeper came down and shouted that there were buildings on fire in St Patrick's Street. Barry immediately opened the shop for one of the night watchmen, and placed the other one at the window overlooking Robert Street. He also told one of the apprentices to watch out a window overlooking Elbow Lane while he himself went to a window at the front of the building with the other apprentice named Collins.

From his position overlooking the street, Barry saw that Grant's department store was on fire and he observed some police and soldiers with a lorry positioned outside the premises. A short time later, he saw an ambulance rushing down St Patrick's Street and noticed a tram on fire near Mangan's jewellery shop. Groups of armed Auxiliaries were now patrolling the street and Barry saw one of them apparently carrying tins of petrol. He then heard noises as if shutters and glass were being broken. In the light of the flames from Grant's he observed another group of police going down Maylor Street. A short time later, he heard an explosion near the domestic part of Cash's in Maylor Street and saw some girls and men rushing out of the building. He then saw three Auxiliaries pass underneath him, and they started to break the glass at Burton's after which he heard a shout, 'The Munster Arcade next'.

The Munster Arcade was then targeted by another group of Auxiliaries. From his vantage point, Barry saw the shutters on the door being torn off and the glass breaking. A bomb was then thrown into the building which exploded somewhere underneath the domestic quarters. Barry immediately went back and got the rest of the employees together. He then went to the window overlooking Elbow Lane and, observing a group of about ten police-men, he shouted at them that there were women in the building. The Auxiliaries replied by shouting at Barry, 'Hold up your hands, the women are safe, whatever about you'. When Barry informed them that the keys of the building were in his possession, he was ordered to come down and open the door. As Barry and the other staff made their way downstairs, they heard other explosions in the building. When they arrived at the side door the police covered them with revolvers, and ordered them to stand against a nearby gate in Elbow Lane. When they were lined up Mrs Gaffney, the housekeeper, asked an Auxiliary officer to let her go back and put on some clothes but he refused saying, 'No, madam, you didn't consider us, we will not consider you'.

While they were being detained, Barry and the others saw an armed police officer with a muffler up to his eyes enter the Munster Arcade carrying 'two heavy looking bags'. A short time later they saw what Barry later described as 'gushes of flames' erupt in the building. As the flames spread through the building Barry and the others were released. They quickly set off towards George's Street in search of shelter but were ordered back by some Auxiliaries who fired a few rounds at them. They then endeavoured to go towards the Victoria Hotel, but encountered yet another group of Auxiliaries who ordered them back. Eventually they managed to get to Marlborough Street where they found refuge in one of the buildings.[116]

There was also considerable activity on Grand Parade around that time. One resident of the avenue later described how at around 9.50 p.m. he heard the sounds of shots and explosions and, looking out his window, he observed the flames from the fire at Grant's. He also witnessed a number of partly dressed people who resided in houses near Grant's leaving their homes carrying bags and other possessions in their hands:

Suddenly three soldiers appeared, one of them wearing a civilian coat. This one in the black coat gave a loud order in a distinct tone of command: 'Get inside'. He spoke with a foreign accent. Some of the people ran, but others, not realising what was happening, remained until, with the giving of the order for the second or third time, he fired shots from his revolver through Hilser's jewellers shop. They then pulled down the shutters and smashed the glass window. The three then looted a little, being helped by Black and Tans who also arrived on the scene. When curfew lorries appeared on the Grand Parade, these looters dodged, three going inside Miss O'Driscoll's door, which is alongside the Central Boot Stores. The lorries went away, and the looters again returned to Hilser's.[117]

Sometime before ten o'clock Superintendent Alfred Hutson, now back on duty at Sullivan's Quay having recovered from his hip injury, received a report that a number of houses at Dillon's Cross were on fire. He immediately contacted the Grattan Street fire station and ordered them to deal with the situation. Five firemen were detailed to take the motor ambulance to Dillon's Cross and one of them later recalled what happened next:

We at once drove out the ambulance, and in five minutes were at Patrick's Street, where we saw Grant's on fire. It was then well alight and too big to be managed by us, so we decided to go at once to Sullivan's Quay for assistance. At the corner of Princes Street and Patrick's Street we stopped on seeing between forty and fifty civilians, well dressed, walking in a body in the middle of the road. They were close to us, marching in step and had revolvers in their hands. At the side of this body of men were four or five men in khaki uniform coats with Glengarry caps. I got down walked towards them and shouted, 'We are firemen'. They halted. 'Where are you going to?' I was asked. In my opinion the speaker had an English accent. I replied, 'To Sullivan's Quay, to turn out the fire brigade'. A man answered me, 'All right. Take your time, you'll have a few more in a minute' ... We then drove to Sullivan's Quay, where we found the fire brigade ready and their appliances on the road. We drove – two horse reels, fire escape, and ambulance – to Grant's, and worked at the fire there. After I was working about half-an-hour near Mutton Lane, at the side of Grant's, I saw the same crowd of men coming along Patrick's Street in the same direction as before ... They stopped for a short time and were speaking to the police and military. They then turned about and went down Patrick's Street in the direction of Patrick's Bridge.[118]

At 10.30 p.m. Hutson received a report that Grant's in the city centre was also on fire. His first action was to contact the military at Victoria Barracks to ask them to take their hose reel and stand pipes at the barrack gate down to Dillon's Cross at once to enable him to devote all his resources to fighting the fire in the city centre. However, no notice was taken of this request and it put Hutson in an impossible position. He did not have enough resources to deal with all the fires simultaneously so he would have to make choices – some fires he would fight, others he could not.

He immediately mobilised his men and rushed to St Patrick's Street. When he arrived at Grant's he noticed that the fire had made considerable headway and the flames were coming through the roof. He knew if the fire managed to spread to the English Market at the rear of Grant's then a major conflagration would erupt as the entire area was constructed primarily of timber.

While he was dealing with this fire, Hutson received word from the town clerk at 11.30 p.m. that the Munster Arcade was on fire and within minutes it was also confirmed that Cash's department store was in flames as well. These two buildings were on the eastern side of St Patrick's Street, near St Patrick's Bridge, and Hutson immediately dispatched all available members and appliances to fight the rapidly spreading inferno. A number of firemen later testified that crown forces impeded their attempts to combat the fires by intimidating them, cutting their hoses and/or driving lorries over the hoses. One of these firemen later recalled what happened when he arrived in St Patrick's Street:

We were useless. They were cutting the hoses and they were firing all around them. There was one man, Tim Ahern's son ... about six foot two, a bloody fine fellow. He was on top of Cash's up a ladder. He was ordered down by a Black and Tan with a bomb in his hand. He was after firing at him previous to that. He was told he would either get this, or get down, and that meant that that fire went on. It was worse than if a fellow was out in Flanders, or many other battlefield.[119]

Accounts of the burning provided by other firemen reflected the general mayhem of the night and the danger to those trying to fight the flames:

I started work about 1.30 a.m. on Sunday. I was helping the firemen at Grant's and went up the escape with Captain Hutson. At about 2 a.m. as I was going up the escape with the hose in my hand, an officer – he was an officer of the Gordon's, and quite young – came out of Market Lane, he was very drunk. He fired twice at me and I threw myself on the ground, and while I was there he discharged another four chambers of his revolver.[120]

While Hutson and this man escaped uninjured other firemen were not so fortunate. One fire-fighter who was working a line of hose on St Patrick's Street later testified that, 'there was firing all round me as I was working at the fire [and] I was hit in the right hand and left ear by bullets and had to be taken in the ambulance to the North Infirmary.'[121] Another who was working the fire engine on Merchant's Quay in the early hours of Sunday morning recalled, 'At about 1.30 a.m. on Monday morning just as I was feeding the boiler, a bullet was fired at me from the direction of St Patrick's Bridge, and injured my nose.'[122]

The arrival of the fire brigade failed to deter the crown forces who seemed hell bent on destroying the centre of Cork. At around

11 p.m. a guest who was staying in the Victoria Hotel was watching events unfold in St Patrick's Street from the attic window of the hotel and recalled hearing glass smashing and a bomb exploding on St Patrick's Street after which a voice with a distinct English accent shouted, 'We'll finish old Cork'.[123]

By now, the *Examiner* reporter, Alan Ellis, was out on St Patrick's Street and shortly after Hutson arrived on the scene he managed to have a few words with him. 'He told me bluntly that all the fires were being deliberately started by incendiary bombs, and in several cases, he had seen soldiers pouring cans of petrol into buildings and setting them alight'. Ellis then made his way towards St Patrick's Bridge and:

On the bridge I saw a deserted tram, set on fire. This was the very one for St. Luke's Cross. 'My last tram home!' was one selfish thought that came into my mind. Anyhow I was not thinking of my lift home any more. I wanted to see as much as I could before going back to the office. Lorries full of regular soldiers, members of the Oxfordshire Regiment, were moving along Merchant's Quay. A crowd of them stood in front of Wickham's shop, which sold primus stoves, on Merchant's Quay. There was little discipline among them. The soldiers were yelling abuse at anyone they saw and now and then firing off a round into the air. Any stragglers were now being halted, searched, and threatened.[124]

In the meantime, the members of the fire brigade were making valiant efforts to contain and extinguish the fires on St Patrick's Street but, despite their best efforts, the flames had rapidly spread to a number of adjoining buildings. By the early hours of Sunday, 12 December, the blaze in the Munster Arcade had spread to Egan's Jewellers, Sunner's, Forrests', the Dartry Dye Company, Saxone Shoe Company, Burton's Tailors, Thomson's and Cudmore's.

Tomás MacCurtain

Courtesy Cork Public Museum

Terence MacSwiney

Courtesy Cork Public Museum

Seán O'Hegarty

Courtesy Cork Public Museum

Donal O'Callaghan

Courtesy Cork Public Museum

Capt. Florence O'Donoghue

Courtesy Breda O'Donoghue Lucci

Josaphine Brown

Courtesy Breda O'Donoghue Lucci

Bishop Danial Cohalan

Courtesy Cork Public Museum

Fr Dominic O'Connor

Courtesy Cork Public Museum

General Crozier inspecting
Auxiliary recruits

Authors' collection

Lord French and General Tudor inspecting a company of
Auxiliaries on parade

Authors' collection

The arrival of the first members of K Coy Auxiliary Division RIC at the Great Southern and Western Railway Station at Lower Glanmire Road

Courtesy *Irish Examiner* [ref: 7b]

Below: group of crown forces comprising members of the Auxiliary Division, RIC, British army and Black and Tans on the Coal Quay, December 1920

Authors' collection

Volunteers who conducted the Dillons Cross ambush

Courtesy of the O'Mahony family

Seán Healy

James O'Mahony

Capt. Seán O'Donoghue

Agustine O'Leary

Michael Kenny

Michael Baylor

The remains of Sunner's Chemist on Patrick Street [left] and Cashman's Wine Merchants on Cook Street [right]

Courtesy of *Irish Examiner*

Smouldering ruins on Patrick Street viewed from Cook Street

Courtesy of *Irish Examiner [ref: 303]*

Temporary offices established by Wm. Egan and Sons and the Munster Arcade after the burning

Courtesy of *Irish Examiner* [ref: 303]

*Funeral of Volunteer Jeremiah Delany passing through Patrick Street
on its way to St Finbarr's cemetery*

Courtesy of *Irish Examiner*

Horse drawn hose reel used by Cork Fire Brigade during the burning of Cork

Courtesy of Pat Poland

Capt. Alfred Hutson, superintendent Cork Fire Brigade

Courtesy of Pat Poland

Capt. Myers, superintendent Dublin Fire Brigade

Courtesy of Pat Poland

British army tank demolishing the ruins of Brian Dillion House

Courtesy of Cork Public Museum

Volunteer Cornelius Delany   *Volunteer Jeremiah Delany*

Courtesy of Cork Public Museum

Canon Thomas J. Magner   *Volunteer Tadhg Crowley*

Courtesy of Fr Donal O'Donovan

Alan Ellis, a critical witness to the burning of Cork, and his son Peter Berresford Ellis

Courtesy of Peter Berresford Ellis

The fire in Cash's had spread to the Lee Cinema, Roches Stores, Lee Boot Company, Connell & Company, Scully's, Wolfe's and O'Sullivan's. Before long these buildings were totally consumed by fire. The night sky over the city had now turned crimson red, black smoke billowed high, filling the air with soot. The streets were awash with water that had poured out of the cut hoses and all sorts of debris was scattered on the pavements.

Many witnesses later testified to the widespread looting carried out by crown forces during the night and the St Patrick's Street resident who earlier had observed the looting of Evan's bookstore had remained at his window while the fires blazed. Around 10.30 p.m. he watched as seven men in uniform approached Mangan's jewellers:

I then heard the smashing of heavy glass and noise as if it was being walked on. Looking out again I saw a large number moving about inside Mangan's, with the aid of electric torch lamps. One man dressed in complete policeman's uniform, was running to and fro outside in a very nervous manner, as if on watch for those inside … The party were inside for upwards of three-quarters of an hour, the lights inside going here and there, and loud noise of smashing of glass. Then they came out. Some dressed in civilian clothes, with light trench coats, some in complete policeman's uniform, numbering about five, and totalling in all about a dozen men. They had large suitcases, a few had small ones in their hands, and appeared heavily laden. They proceeded calmly in the direction of Cash's.[125]

An ex-British army officer who had been forced to seek shelter in a hotel on MacCurtain Street (formerly King Street) also described how:

from 11 p.m. onwards Auxiliaries and Black and Tans, also RIC came up King Street from Bridge Street direction laden with suitcases, travelling rugs, coats and hats, and proceeded towards Summerhill. They came and went in batches. As it got later the majority of the men I saw were drunk and some staggered very much'.[126]

Crown forces also revisited the home of Sinn Féin Alderman Coughlan that night. His wife, Ellen, gave this account of the terror that was again inflicted upon her household while Cork burned:

At 1 a.m. on the night (morning) of December 12, 1920, I heard a knocking at the door. A stone then came crashing through a window pane in a front room ... probably on account of the delay in opening the door. The girl staying with me went down and opened the door. Shortly after, a man rushed up the stairs and entered my bedroom. He seemingly knew his way. He was dressed in a trench coat and military khaki cap, and carried a revolver at his right side. He demanded to know where Mr. Coughlan was. From his speech, build and height, I believe him to be the same officer who raided the house a fortnight previous, armed and disguised, looking for my husband to shoot him.

My husband fortunately was not there on the occasion. I said I could not tell him where he was, as I did not know. He moved over close to me and behind my left shoulder, and demanded my husband's whereabouts again. It was of no use. He searched the room for a few minutes. He then said, 'Get me those papers, invoices, etc. belonging to the place. Demanding the keys of the safe, I told him they may be below, and he rushed down and returned with the little girl whom I told to get the keys out of my pocket. When he got the keys he went below. After some minutes below he returned to me, and searched my coat where the keys had been. Finding nothing, he turned to me and said, 'Where's the money? Where do you keep it?' I said, 'It's in the bank'. He then said, 'What about tonight's takings?' I said, 'The boy took it home with him'. He growled and said, 'I must burn now'. I said 'God help us, will you give us time to take out the children'. He said nothing. My two children, aged 5½ and 7½ years, were in bed in the room at the time. He paused for a while, and holding his revolver up, said, 'If Mr Coughlan is not back within a week, I'll burn the place. Do you hear? Are you aware of that?' Repeating this threat a second time, he left, and I saw him no more.[127]

As the terror continued Alan Ellis made his way to the offices of the *Cork Examiner* on St Patrick's Street where he found to his surprise that:

Jack Healy, the editor was already there. My surprise was because there was no Sunday edition of the newspaper and no need for the editor to be there. A general picture was emerging. The Auxiliaries and Black and Tans, supported by some regular troops, many wearing scarves over their faces, were firing shops in the Grand Parade and Washington Street. A jewellers shop in Washington Street had been looted, as well as shops along Marlboro' Street. Witnesses saw soldiers carrying away kitbags full of booty ... Having checked with Mr. Healy, I left the office to see what else I could observe. Alexander Pope wrote that 'fools rush in where angels fear to tread.' Had I been wiser, I might not have ventured out again.

As I reached the bottom of Abbey Street, I was stopped by a patrol of the Buckinghamshire Light Infantry. In spite of protests, I was bundled into a car, a 'Lancia' I think. At first I was taken to King Street RIC barracks, next to the Grosvenor Hotel. There was some mention of 'a muddle' for I was pushed back into the vehicle and was driven to the Union Quay RIC barracks. The place was filled with Auxies who seemed to look at me with some unpleasant smiles of what, I thought, was anticipation. I waved my pass and identification at the sergeant in charge but he 'had his orders' and I was held until a young lieutenant of the regulars, no older than myself but wearing a Military Cross ribbon, interrogated me. He looked embarrassed, especially when I asked why the military were setting fire to the city. He simply muttered something about the Auxiliaries being 'out of control'.[128]

But the events of the night were not yet complete, nor were they confined exclusively to arson and looting. At a farm at Dublin Hill on the north side of the city lived a well known republican family called Delany. Two brothers, Jeremiah and Cornelius, had joined the Volunteers becoming members of F Company, 1st Battalion, Cork No. 1 Brigade and were known to the authorities in that regard. Daniel Delany, the head of the family, related what happened in the early hours of Sunday morning:

About 2 a.m. a number of men came to my door and demanded admission in a loud voice, and beat the door harshly. I opened the door, and they called me out. The man who seemed to be in command asked if I was a Sinn Féiner. I answered, 'I don't understand you'. He then said, 'Are you interested in politics?' I answered, 'I am an old man and not interested in anything'. He then asked, 'Who is inside?' I said, 'Nobody but my family'. 'Can I see them?' said he. 'Certainly,' I said. 'They are in bed'. He asked me to show them up. Then at least eight men entered the house and went upstairs. A large number remained outside, as I could hear them moving and see them in the yard. The men who went upstairs entered my sons' bedroom, and said in a harsh voice, 'Get up out of that'. I was in the room with them. My sons got up and stood at the bedside. They asked them if their name was Delany.

My sons answered, 'Yes'. At that moment I heard distinctly two or more shots, and my two boys fell immediately. My brother-in-law, William Dunlea, who was sleeping in the same room in another bed was fired on by the same party and wounded in two places. My brother-in-law is over sixty years of age. As far as I could see, they wore long overcoats, and spoke with a strong English accent.[129]

One of Daniel Delany's daughters had been awoken by the knocking on the door and later recalled that:

I arose and went towards my brothers' bedroom. I saw a number of men going downstairs, their backs towards me. I entered my brothers' room, and saw my brother, Jeremiah, lying on the floor; he was not then dead, his lips were moving. My brother Con was lying in the bed in a pool of blood. I ran out and got the crucifix. I asked my brother to kiss the crucifix. He did so, and put up his hand to keep silent. I then presented the crucifix to Jeremiah, and asked him to kiss it. As I did so, he turned his head towards me and I put the crucifix to his lips. He died immediately. I left the room to get bandages. I got some, and left them in the room. As I was going downstairs to go for a priest and doctor, I met a man coming towards me with a revolver and torchlight. I asked him where he was going, put my two hands to his chest and besought him, for God's sake, not to go up as they were all dead. He persisted in his efforts and said, 'Is there anybody belonging to me up there', in a foreign accent. My father answered, 'Nobody but dead men'. He then left. I followed him to the door. He said something to a number of men who were downstairs, and they left the house. As I was crossing the road, just outside the house going for a nurse, I saw a motor car on the road, about 150 yards away. The lights of the car were facing me, in the direction of my father's house. Before I got out of bed I heard a motor car stopping outside the gate leading to the yard.

I went to the nearest telephone and rang up the fire station, and asked them to send an ambulance. I got a reply stating that there was no ambulance available, that there were a number of houses on fire in Patrick's Street, and that the men were afraid to go out as there was considerable firing in Patrick's Street. It was then about 3.30 a.m. We procured a priest from the Presbytery (North Cathedral) at 4 a.m. He advised me to telephone again for the ambulance. We did so, and at 8 a.m. the Union ambulance arrived and took my brother Con to the Mercy Hospital.[130]

Why the Delany household was raided that night remains unclear. One theory suggests that the Auxiliary patrol ambushed at Dillon's Cross might well have been on its way to the Delany farm to arrest the brothers for their Volunteer activities and this raid was just a continuation of that original mission. A second theory suggests that in the aftermath of the ambush the crown forces used bloodhounds to track the escaping Volunteers and, as they searched the scene, a cap belonging to one of the ambush party was recovered. This had apparently been dropped while the Volunteers were escaping through the Glen and, when given to the dogs, provided a scent which led directly to the Delany farm where O'Donoghue had hidden the unused bombs.[131] The fact that bloodhounds were used makes the latter explanation more probable.

Meanwhile, Alan Ellis was still incarcerated at Union Quay RIC Barracks and had been trying, unsuccessfully, to convince his captors that he was not actually dangerous:

The officer checked with the *Examiner* office by phone but I had to give another reference, so I gave them the phone number of my 'respectable' cousin William [who] apparently endorsed that I was not a 'suspicious character' and so I was released.[132] No one offered me transport home. I was released sometime after three o'clock in the morning. There was still gunfire in the city. I heard it not far away at Bandon railway station and my idiocy drew me along the quay to see what was going on. I found a unit of the city fire brigade actually pinned down by gunfire. When I asked who was firing on them, they said it was Black and Tans who had broken into the nearby City Hall next to the station. One fireman told me that he had also seen 'men in uniform' carrying cans of petrol into the Hall from the very barracks on Union Quay that I just been released from. Around four o'clock there was a tremendous explosion. The Tans had not only placed petrol in the building but also detonated high explosives. The City Hall and adjoining Carnegie Library, with its hundreds of priceless volumes, was suddenly a sea of flames.[133]

When Hutson received word of these latest outbreaks, he dispatched seven of his men to fight the fires but once again they were subjected to intimidation by crown forces who fired shots in their direction. But as Alan Ellis later wrote, they soon tired of this activity: 'Instead they turned off the fire hydrant and refused to let the fire crews have any access to water. Protests were met with laughter and abuse. Soon after six o'clock the tower of the City Hall crashed into the ruins below'.[134]

With the City Hall and Carnegie Library consumed by fire, the final act of arson and looting now took place at the Murphy Brothers' clothes shop on Washington Street near St Augustine's priory. At around 6 a.m. one of the order residing in the priory was awakened by the sound of breaking glass coming from the street below. Looking out his window, he saw a policeman stooped over what appeared to be a bundle of clothes on the pavement outside Murphy's shop window. A man from across the road had also witnessed what he described as 'six men – three of them dressed in policeman's heavy overcoats and caps – and an officer in khaki uniform breeches and ordinary military cap' outside Murphy's shop. Unlike the Augustinian, he observed the men loot the shop and then set it on fire. He shouted a warning to the priory across the road. The Augustinian who was watching out his window was quick to react:

> I immediately phoned Union Quay Police Barracks for police protection, telling them that three men were looting Murphy Brothers … and that we feared they would break into our church … They referred me to the Bridewell and I got what I thought was a giggle from them for my pains. They promised to send assistance. I also phoned the fire brigade, and they sent along a man.[135]

However, before the fireman arrived, five members of the order went down onto the street and tackled the flames themselves using buckets of water. The fire was extinguished around 6.30 a.m. and the Augustinians went back to the priory for breakfast. Around a half hour later, they heard further noises from the shop and discovered that three policemen were again looting the premises. One of them was seen carrying a pink golf coat and before they departed one of his fellow officers looked at the Augustinians and said, 'That's for his young lady'.[136]

As dawn broke on Sunday, 12 December, the centre of the city of Cork was covered in a cloud of smoke and the streets were awash with a black, mud-like substance, formed from a mixture of soot, ashes and water. While exhausted groups of firemen were still hosing down the smouldering remains of the fires, a number of citizens found the courage to venture from their homes en route to Mass, their place of employment, or just to view the destruction that had been wrought upon their city. The lamplighters usually came on duty at 7 a.m. at that time of the year to extinguish the street lights. One lamplighter whose route took him to City Hall left his home on the north side of the River Lee:

> I proceeded down Pope's Quay and over Patrick's Bridge and the first thing that took my eye was something in the middle of Patrick's Street just by the fireman's rest. I went over out of curiosity and it was a tram burnt to a cinder. I went down Merchant's Street by the light of the fire, of course there was no other light you see. As I was going down Merchant's Street I met one of my comrades. 'Where are you going?' he said. I told him that I was going to City Hall. 'There's no City Hall there,' he said, 'it was burned down'.[137]

Another man was returning home having been on night duty in the Glanmire railway station and, having heard early mass in St Patrick's church, he made his way to the city centre:

> I walked up to Patrick's Street. And a short distance down that street I saw a heap of books on the pavement. Seán from the chapel was with me. We picked up some and examined them. We were inclined to take some with us but ... didn't and threw them back on the street. Walking down further to the junction of Marlborough Street we saw a couple of lads and this man and woman who were bringing a mattress through a window when what I took to be an RIC man came over and hit the woman over the neck with a gun and they decamped leaving the mattress on the street with the other rubble that was knocking around at the time; hoses, bricks, tiles and all other sorts of stuff.[138]

Then, in the purest of ironies, many of the city's children emerged from a night of fear and confusion and began to play amidst the wreckage and debris. One later recalled his experiences:

> We went down Patrick's Street, myself and a chap named Thomas

Sullivan. I walked down about fifty yards and I spotted a little three wheel cycle and, as it was coming on to Christmas, I thought what a lovely present it would make. I was making an attempt to save it from being burned when I got a boot on the backside and I was sent off about my business. After that we went down where the ESB showrooms are at present and we were rummaging amongst the debris and … we saw a hole in the wall. Sullivan, being a bit stronger than me, went in and came out with a huge parcel of pipes, tobacco, organs and souvenirs. We kept the mouth organs, but sold the pipes and tobacco – about thirty shillings for 'picture' money.[139]

For Alan Ellis it was finally time to make his way home to grab some much needed sleep:

Exhausted by that time, I found a wandering fellow reporter from the *Cork Examiner* who gave me a lift back to Sunday's Well on his motorcycle. At least, it being Sunday I could have a few hours sleep before going into the office to see if Jack Healy would believe the copy that I was going to deliver.[140]

However there would be little time for sleep. Within a few hours, Ellis would be on his feet again reporting on the fall out from the night's events.

10

AFTERMATH

As the citizens of Cork emerged from their homes that Sunday morning it was difficult to come to terms with the scale of destruction which lay before them; the centre of their city was effectively destroyed. The foul smell of smouldering ruins mingled with the crisp air of a winter's morning. Florrie O'Donoghue later recalled that:

> Many familiar landmarks were gone forever – where whole buildings had collapsed here and there a solitary wall leaned at some crazy angle from its foundation. The streets ran with sooty water, the footpaths were strewn with broken glass and debris, ruins smoked and smouldered and over everything was the all pervasive smell of burning.[141]

The fire brigade – although completely exhausted – continued to pour water on the debris to prevent the fires from re-igniting. Recognising their inability to continue, especially if new fires erupted, Lord Mayor Dónal O'Callaghan sent a request for assistance to his fellow mayors in the cities of Dublin and Limerick. Dublin responded immediately by sending a motor pump by train, together with seven men, under the personal supervision of its chief fire officer, Captain Myers. Limerick sent a detachment with a horse-drawn steam pump, by road.

The British army in Victoria Barracks were also busy that morning. General Strickland made a note in his pocket diary: 'a desperate night. City Hall and part of Patrick Street burnt, we suspect by Special Coy RC. Many people asking if it's safe to go out'.[142] Major F. R. Eastwood, the brigade major of the 17th Infantry Brigade, sat down in his office to compile the daily curfew report for Cork city for the night of 11/12 December. It read as follows:

1.   Three arrests were made.

2.   At 22.00 hours, Grant & Co., Patrick Street was found to be on fire. Warning was sent to all fire brigades.

3.   At about 00.30 hours, Cash & Co. and the Munster Arcade were reported on fire.

4.   At 05.30 hours the majority of the troops were withdrawn, and the remainder at 08.00 hours.

5.   Explosions were heard at 00.15 hours, but were not located. No shots were fired by the troops.

F. R. EASTWOOD, Major.

Brigade Major, 17th Infantry Brigade,

Cork, 12.12.20.[143]

At the Bishop's Place in Farranferris, Dr Cohalan decided to use the homily at twelve o'clock mass in the North Cathedral to comment on recent events. While the congregation might have expected some comment on the burning of the city, they received instead his observations on the Volunteer's military campaign:

Murder is murder and arson is arson, whether committed by the agents of the government or by members of the Volunteer organisation and it is the duty of a bishop to denounce murder and arson and all crimes from whatever source they come. And, today, in the presence of the destruction of our city, I ask you to consider reasonably the subject of the murders, of the arsons, of the kidnappings and the ambushes with which unfortunately we have got too familiar.

It is a safe exploit to murder a policeman from behind a screen and until reprisals began, there was no danger to the general community. But, even leaving aside the moral aspect of the question for the moment, what has the country gained by the murder of policemen? Some republicans spoke of such and such districts of the country being delivered from British sway when policemen were murdered and barracks burned. It was a narrow view, and who will now mention any district that has been delivered from British rule by the murder of the old RIC men and the burning of the barracks? No, the killing of the RIC men was murder and the burning of the RIC barracks simply the destruction of Irish property. I might say that reprisals began with the murder of Lord Mayor MacCurtain, and now it is like the devil's competition between some members of the Republican Army and the agents of the crown in feats of murder or arson.

Recently ambushes have taken place with serious loss of life. I would like to say this about the ambushes, leaving out the question of their moral aspect: the ambushers come to a place from no one knows where and when their work is done, they depart, no one knows to what destination. There is not much risk to the ambushers personally. But by this time, boys and men taking part in ambushes must know that by their criminal acts they are exposing perhaps a whole countryside, perhaps a whole town or city to the danger of terrible reprisals; that when they depart and disperse in safety they are leaving the lives and property of a number of innocent people unprotected and undefended to the fury of reprisals at the hands of the servants of the government. This is not very valiant. And then, over and above all, there is the moral aspect of these ambushes. Let there be no doubt about it, these ambushes are murderous and every life taken in an ambush is a murder. There is even danger of becoming familiar with murder, of simply considering a successful ambush as a nice exploit brought off, of thinking no more of shooting a policeman than of shooting game or a wild animal. I am afraid some of our young men have got wrong views from people who should know better. I have repeatedly, here in the cathedral and in the several parishes during visitations, condemned these murders. 'He who will not hear the church, let him be to thee as the heathen or the publican!' Notwithstanding repeated condemnations of murder and repeated warnings, terrible crimes have been committed these past few weeks. As a result of a terrible ambush last night at Dillon's Cross the city has suffered, I think, as much damage at the hands of servants of the Government as Dublin suffered during the rebellion of 1916. It is all very well talking grandiloquently of the city being under the care and solicitude of the Republican Army. The city is nearly a ruin and the ruin followed on the murderous ambush at Dillon's Cross.[144]

The bishop then spoke directly to those involved in the republican movement and declared:

If any section or member of the Volunteer organisation refuse to hear the church's teaching about murder, there is no remedy but the extreme remedy of excommunication from the church. And I will certainly issue a decree of excommunication against anyone who, after this notice, shall take part in an ambush or a kidnapping or attempted murder or arson.[145]

The bishop's remarks presented the majority of rank and file Volunteers with a serious moral dilemma. Most Volunteers were devout Catholics who firmly believed in the justness of their military actions. Now they were to be cut adrift by their church and left to wonder what their God might say in the event of a premature meeting with him. A difficult time for the Volunteers had just got immeasurably worse.

In the meantime, Alan Ellis only managed to snatch a few hours sleep before a messenger arrived from the *Cork Examiner* to tell him that the editor needed him to cover what he believed was a 'still breaking story'. When he got there he discovered that the editor had spent the entire night in his office. He also discovered that because of the previous night's events there were no trams running and the city's gas supply had been shut down. Having been at boiling point a few hours previously, the city now began to freeze as the sun went down.

The chief reporter dispatched Ellis to a specially convened meeting of Cork Corporation which was being held that afternoon at the Corn Exchange.[146] Dónal O'Callaghan presided and the following members attended: Aldermen J. J. Walsh, William Stockley, Denis Lucy, Tadhg Barry, and Charles Coughlan; and councillors James Allen, Thomas Daly, Barry M. Egan, Sir Edward Fitzpatrick, Seán French, Thomas Forde, John Good, Michael Ó'Cuill, Seán O'Leary, Micheal J. O'Riordan, Liam Russell, John Sheehan, Professor Alfred O'Rahilly and Sir John Scott. It was immediately agreed to suspend standing orders and to pass the estimates for 1921 submitted by the city treasurer. Sir John Scott then moved that the corporation, 'Welcome the efforts which are now being made by some of our fellow countrymen with a view to securing peace in Ireland' and 'offer their cooperation to his Grace, the Archbishop of Tuam in his wise suggestion to have a truce proclaimed so that peace and goodwill may again reign in Ireland'. Alderman Barry seconded this motion but only 'for the purpose of discussion'. Councillor Barry Egan then moved the following amendment which was seconded by Councillor Ó'Cuill:

We, the Corporation of Cork, affirm once more that the Irish nation is fighting for its very existence against an unscrupulous enemy, but is desirous of an honourable peace consistent with its position as a sovereign state, and we express our undiminished confidence in our elected representatives who alone are authorised to speak on our behalf. We proclaim our unaltered determination to seek or sanction no truce or peace save such an international agreement as is arranged between Dáil Éireann (the Irish government) and the British government.[147]

This motion was passed after Alderman Barry withdrew as a seconder for the original motion.

The Corporation next agreed to form an unemployment committee in an attempt to alleviate the now widespread unemployment caused by the burning of the city centre. The committee comprised: five members of the Corporation, two representatives from the Harbour Board, two from each Chamber of Commerce, two from the Irish Trade and Labour Council, two from the Transport Workers Union, two from the Employers Federation, two from the executive of Sinn Féin and two from the Farmer's Union.

The members also resolved that the lord mayor should send a telegram to the pope and to representatives of the European nations and the USA, drawing their attention to the state of affairs existing in Ireland, particularly in the city of Cork, and asking for the intervention of their respective governments. The members then passed a vote of thanks to the councils of Dublin and Limerick for sending firemen and equipment to Cork to help fight the fires.

Once these matters had been attended to J. J. Walsh then declared there was one more matter he wished to bring to the attention of the Corporation:

The city of Cork has been going through a terrible time in which the people have suffered almost beyond endurance. This should have raised resentment in the position of his lordship the bishop of Cork yet not a single word of protest was uttered, and today, after the city has been decimated, he saw no better course than to add insult to injury. The seriousness of the utterances of his lordship was that they would be used for propagandist purposes and in such a way as to blackmail the Irish people by holding them up as the evil-doers and not those who were responsible for what had been done.[148]

Walsh went on to urge those present to express some regret or resentment at 'the untimely and unfair action his lordship had adopted'. While acknowledging that this would be a 'strong and unusual course' to pursue, he felt that the council in session was the place to express such condemnation and to 'put themselves and the citizens right before the world'. Sir John Scott replied that he had not seen the bishop's letter but that he knew him well and was certain he would not do anything 'against the wishes of his people'. This in turn led Councillor Ó'Cuill to remark, 'He is really your bishop now, Sir John – he is no longer mine'. Alderman Barry seconded Walsh's suggestion. The lord mayor declared he too agreed with the sentiments expressed by Walsh and that, while the people of Cork seemed able to bear up under all the 'ruffianism' it was possible to inflict on them, it was terrible to think that when they woke up to find their city in ruins there was no word of condemnation from the bishop. He went on to say that 'the ruin caused would run into millions and thousands of people were thrown out of employment but there was no condemnation of that save words that add to the powers of terrorism possessed by those who had done the damage'. However, he went on to state that in his opinion it was scarcely a matter that the Corporation, composed as it was of mixed parties, could deal with:

Were they considering merely an expression of opinion from his lordship they would be entitled to do so, and would do so with wisdom and judgement, but in the present case they were face to face with a decree of excommunication, and while the matter must be dealt with I think it should be dealt with in another way rather than by a resolution of the corporation.[149]

He continued by saying that the matter should really be dealt with by individuals, by a statement or pronunciation by some of the representatives, as this would not bind the corporation or the city and it would then be up to other members of the public to endorse or differ from what was said. Walsh declared that while he was willing to accept the lord mayor's suggestion, he did feel that if the matter was put before council it would be passed. He also stated that he was satisfied the bishop's statement had met with general condemnation among the priests and people of Cork. Councillor Good asked if it was necessary to defer the issue, stating that the actions of the crown forces during the past week had incensed the people of Cork and he felt the bishop had made a 'great mistake' interfering in such matters. Councillor Ó'Cuill again displayed his contempt for Bishop Cohalan by retorting that 'he stands now only where his people always stood – in the wrong'.

Professor O'Rahilly said he felt the matter was an ecclesiastical one and as such they should not interfere. He believed it was a matter for the bishops of Ireland who, at their last meeting, had made an entirely different statement declaring that the English had no right to their country and if there was any pronouncement which so asserted then that pronouncement was wrong. The lord mayor finally brought the discussion to a close by saying that as far as he was concerned 'the fortunate thing [now] was that the people could do what they had always done – follow their own consciences'.[150]

The following evening, 13 December, the burning of Cork was debated in the House of Commons. T. P. O'Connor, the only Irish Party MP to sit for an English constituency (the Scotland division of Liverpool) opened the debate by asking the government for particulars on the number of buildings burned, the value of property destroyed and the number of persons, if any, killed and wounded. He also asked if the government had discovered 'the authors of this series of crimes', and whether they would be brought to trial at the earliest possible moment. He was followed by Lieutenant Commander Kenworthy, who asked for information concerning the Dillon's Cross ambush.

In reply, Sir Hamar Greenwood informed the House that he hadn't yet received a full or even written report regarding the incidents in Cork but the facts had been communicated to him by telegram. He said that twelve Auxiliaries had been wounded in the attack [at Dillon's Cross] – five or six of them seriously – and that one had since died of his wounds. He also stated that at around the same time attacks had been made on other parties of Auxiliaries in the city. Then, at about 9.30 p.m., the Cork police had received a message stating that a fire had broken out in the large premises of Alexander Grant on St Patrick's Street and a short time later reports had been received that both Cash's and Co. and the Munster Arcade were on fire. He went on to state that:

The fire brigade were immediately brought up under military escort and the police forces quartered in all parts of the city were dispatched to the scene under the command of the District Inspector. Strenuous efforts were made by the fire brigade to extinguish the flames but despite their best efforts the flames spread to a number of buildings including the City Hall, Carnegie Library and fifteen other large business premises. The extent of the damage and destruction caused has not yet been ascertained.

The police and the military gave all possible assistance to the fire brigade in checking the flames. A certain amount of looting took place around 2 and 3 a.m. and the police made a baton charge on a crowd of about a hundred people engaged in looting and made several arrests.[151]

When Greenwood informed the House that it was not known who had started the fires, the opposition benches erupted in jeers which led to an outburst from the government benches. Greenwood then carried on by declaring:

I must protest most vigorously against the suggestion, without any evidence, that these fires were started by forces of the Crown. There is no evidence to this effect and it is obvious to anyone that a fire of this kind is the only possible argument that is now used against the government's policy in Ireland.[152]

Kenworthy then stood up and asked the secretary if there was any truth in the report carried by the *Times* that 'three civilians named Delany were dragged from their home and shot', or any truth in the other reports carried in papers friendly to the government that 'the hoses of the fire brigade had been cut and that the fire brigade was fired at while extinguishing the fires'. To this Greenwood replied:

There is not an atom of evidence that I know of to that effect. Every available policeman and soldier in Cork was turned out at once and without their assistance the fire brigade could not have gone through the crowds and did the work that they tried to do. There is no evidence of hoses being cut or of forces of the Crown being responsible for these outrages at all.[153]

When Kenworthy again asked who did start the fires, Greenwood said:

> There is some evidence that they were started by incendiary bombs. There are no incendiary bombs in the possession of the forces of the Crown in Ireland. There are incendiary bombs in possession of the Sinn Féiners – and we are seizing them every week.[154]

More speakers then joined the debate. Lieutenant Colonel Walter Guinness asked how long after the ambush did the fires take place. He was followed by Lord Cavendish who asked were not the people of the country and the House entitled to an impartial inquiry into the events in Cork. In reply, Greenwood stood up and said:

> The whole area is under Martial Law. Of course the House is entitled to all the information and I think the best inquiry and the most impartial will be made by the general officer commanding on the spot.[155]

Lieutenant Colonel Guinness then returned to the matter of blame, asking, 'Were the fires simultaneous and was it in any way possible in the time that elapsed since the murderous attacks for the troops to have organised such fires?' In response to the query, Kenworthy shouted, 'not the troops' and Jerimiah MacVeagh immediately followed with, 'Black and Tans'. Greenwood tried to deflect these accusations by replying, 'The attacks on the lorry, according to the evidence before me, was at eight o'clock at a place called Dillon's Cross which is not in the centre of Cork at all'. But MacVeagh, who obviously knew the geography of the city quickly shot back, 'it is within a half mile!' To which the secretary replied:

Yes, within a half mile and there were certain houses from which the police allege bombs were thrown at them at Dillon's Cross which were actually destroyed, and the police have authority to destroy houses from which they are fired at. The fires broke out more or less simultaneously at 9.30 near the centre of the city, and my submission is that the fires in the centre of the city had nothing to do with the attack on the military division half mile from the centre of the city.[156]

When the Irish Party MP Captain William Archer Redmond asked how long it would be before the House had the results of the inquiry which was about to be set up, Greenwood replied:

The GOC in Cork city, in the Munster area under Martial Law proclamation, is now in sole charge and command. He has already issued very drastic orders dealing with looting and burning. He is one of the most distinguished officers in the British army and I have every confidence in him. As to the report of the inquiry – as soon as it is available I shall do my best.[157]

When Redmond again asked how long it would be, Greenwood replied that it was impossible to say. Then, in a reference to the GOC in Cork city, Captain Elliot asked, 'Is this the same man who, after being fired at in a recent outrage, succeeded in preventing reprisals on the part of the troops?' In reply, Greenwood told the House, 'This officer is General Strickland who was recently fired on by several assassins and drove at once to his headquarters and issued orders for no reprisals. He is in command of three thousand troops. It is a tribute to the splendid discipline of the troops'.[158] Upon hearing this statement Mr MacVeagh then stood up and asked the speaker:

Is the right honourable gentleman aware that nobody had suggested that the fires were started by the military but that they were started by forces of the Crown? If Martial Law is in operation in the city and so many thousands of troops and Black and Tans and the RIC concentrated there, how is it that he is unable to detect the malefactors in any fire that was started?[159]

To this Greenwood replied, 'There are not thousands of troops nor thousands of Auxiliaries nor thousands of RIC in Cork'. MacVeagh immediately asked, 'How many are there?' and Greenwood declared, 'I cannot say, but what I can say is that it is obviously to the interests of the government to find the perpetrators of these outrages and I have every confidence in the general officer commanding in doing so'.[160]

In response to a question about an attack against a barracks in Ireland on the previous night, Greenwood informed the House that such an attack did indeed take place and that one RIC constable lost his life and two were wounded. Kenworthy then stood up and, addressing the speaker, declared:

I beg leave to move the adjournment of the House to call attention to the reprisals by burning and shootings in the city of Cork following the ambushing of a party of Auxiliary police within twenty-four hours of the proclamation of Martial Law and the failure of the government to protect life and property in the city of Cork.[161]

In response to this motion, Sir John Butcher asked the speaker:

Is it in order for an honourable member, in view of the answer which has just been given by a responsible minister in charge of Ireland, to found a motion for the adjournment on the allegation that there have been reprisals when there had been no reprisals at all?[162]

He was followed by Mr MacVeagh who asked the speaker if it was a fact that property to the value of £3,000 had been destroyed and that the government was unable to protect property. The speaker then ruled that the motion would be put to the House, leaving out the word 'reprisals'. Forty members rose in support and the adjournment was put down for 8.15 p.m.

When the House reassembled at the appointed time, with the deputy speaker in the chair, Kenworthy stood up and moved the adjournment declaring that:

> We are face to face with an extraordinary state of affairs in Ireland and particularly in the city of Cork. On Friday, the prime minister made a statement in which in one direction, he appeared to have made a step forward, and to have opened the door to peaceful negotiations with the leaders of the majority of the Irish people, and, in another direction he declared that Martial Law would be imposed in certain parts of Ireland. From what I know of recent events in Ireland I believe that the strict application of Martial Law would be far superior to the anarchy and negation of any sort of law that had been ruling since last summer over a great part of the south and west of that country. Martial Law has been proclaimed by the lord lieutenant in the county and city of Cork. A sermon has been preached by the bishop of Cork on Sunday in which he denounced murderous violence on both sides and particularly dwelt on ambushes and the sniping of forces of the crown. He also condemned illegal reprisals on the other side. The Bishop of Cork is by no means the first ecclesiastic in Ireland to condemn these crimes. In fact I think all ecclesiastics in Ireland have denounced murder in Ireland for months past.[163]

Kenworthy went on to describe the events in Cork the previous Saturday night, beginning with the Dillon's Cross ambush. He felt the practice of sending lorry loads of troops along the roads in Ireland without armoured protection was 'questionable' as if the idea was that the troops would terrorise the population. He said it was not a policy the House would agree with. He then mentioned that, according to the *Times*, 'three men named Delany were dragged from their house and murdered' and hoped the chief secretary would give the House full information on the case. Referring to the burning of the city he said the damage done was estimated at £3 million, that two previous attempts had been made to burn the City Hall, and that firemen fighting the fires there on Saturday night had been 'driven out at the point of a revolver'. The Carnegie Library had also been burned and 'what the House wanted to know,' he declared, 'was who had perpetrated the damage?' He went on to inform the House that he had received a letter from a priest in Cork enclosing a cutting from the *Cork Examiner* which said the people of Cork were 'living in a state of terror'. He also said that the suspicion in the south and west of Ireland was that the Anti-Sinn Féin Society and its excesses and outrages were the work of the military, that the Auxiliary police were responsible for what happened in Cork, and that there was strong evidence to suggest the government was responsible for these reprisals.

He then informed the House that he had received a telegram from the lord mayor of Cork, signed by two Sinn Féin MPs:

During the past week men, women and children had been 'held up' in the streets and robbed of all they possessed. That hundreds of shops had been looted, citizens whipped and shot and, it was feared, in some cases burnt alive in their homes. The principal business quarters had been bombed and destroyed by forces of the Crown rendering thousands of the people workless and homeless.[164]

Kenworthy concluded by declaring that he had a right to ask the chief secretary to refute these statements and that the burning of dwelling houses was almost as bad as the shootings. He demanded that this sort of thing be stopped and that real Martial Law, especially in Cork, be put in place. He said General Strickland had stopped reprisals after the attempt on his life and he hoped that he would stop reprisals again – for the credit of the British army. He stated that looters would be shot and he hoped that murderers on both sides would be dealt with using the utmost rigour of the law. 'It was not enough,' he proclaimed, 'for the right honourable gentlemen to declare that these Auxiliary police were gallant ex-officers. There were black sheep in every fighting force'.[165]

Kenworthy's last remarks led to uproar on the government side of the House. One member shouted, 'You are one!' and Charles Jesson told Kenworthy that he 'was a disgrace to the service'. The opposition benches resounded with cries of 'withdraw'; Jesson withdrew his remarks and apologised.[166]

In seconding the motion, James Hogge said that the happenings in Cork, whether they called them reprisals or not, were damaging to the name and honour of England in other parts of the world and that was a serious consideration. William Adamson spoke next and said the events in Cork had been so serious that the public would expect the House to take notice of them. He also said there were those who held the view that, if the Irish situation had been handled in a different manner in recent months, much wanton destruction, murder and terrorism could have been avoided. He further stated that it was up to the House to have the matter inquired into and have responsibility placed on the right shoulders. He said it was in their interest and in the interest of the people of England to appoint a royal commission to inquire into what had happened in Cork.

In response, Sir Hamar Greenwood said that he appreciated what he considered was the 'new atmosphere' in the House in discussing these very difficult questions that arose in Ireland. He deplored the shootings and burnings and any failure – which he did not admit – of the government to protect life and property in Cork or elsewhere but admitted that the protection of life and property would remain difficult until the Sinn Féin conspiracy was crushed at the source. He continued by saying, 'the great calamity in Ireland was not the loss of property but the loss of life' and said it was a reflection on many people that no serious debate was ever raised in the House about reprisals until the burning of a shirt factory in Balbriggan. He regretted that one Auxiliary had lost his life but was glad to report that the eleven who had been wounded were doing well. He also regretted the loss of life of one 'Sinn Féiner' but was glad to say that up to the present there was not the slightest evidence of loss of life due to the fires in Cork except one – a woman looter who was shot. He went on to say that the loss of one life was more important than a city hall being burned down. Referring to the imposition of Martial Law, the chief secretary said it would be administered 'by the commander-in-chief in Ireland and under him by General Strickland who commanded the Munster Division of the Irish forces'. 'Strickland was absolute in his powers', he informed the House, and one example of his absolute powers under Martial Law was that he had issued an order that anyone found looting, burning or attempting either, would be shot.

Greenwood then turned his attention to who was responsible for burning the city. He believed the imposition of Martial Law had nothing to do with it and while he had no evidence as to who had carried out the act, he did not personally believe that forces of the crown were responsible. It was his contention that the forces of the crown had actually saved Cork because when the fire brigade was exhausted the police and military took over their work and were under perfect control. There was no evidence that one of them had caused a single fire of the great conflagration, although he did admit that, following the Dillon's Cross ambush, 'certain small houses were destroyed because from these houses bombs were thrown at the police'. If any member of his Majesty's forces were found guilty of arson he would be treated in accordance with the provisions of Martial Law. He thought the best custodians of the honour of the British army were men like General Strickland and he had more confidence in him than in any tribunal. Referring to the evidence sent to Kenworthy by a 'sporting priest' from Cork, Greenwood said he hoped he would send the name of the priest to General Strickland. Turning to the accusations contained in the telegram received from the Sinn Féin MPs, he said there was not the slightest evidence that any persons had been burned alive. In response to calls for an inquiry, he informed the House that an inquiry had been started that day under the orders of General Strickland and would be finished the next day. He also stated he would wire the general that night asking him to call before his tribunal the lord mayor of Cork, Mr Walsh and Mr Roche. When one member of the House called for 'safe conduct', Greenwood replied that the three would get the safest conduct in Ireland: that of his Majesty's forces. Greenwood then went on to condemn the Sinn Féin members:

> Not one of the three had ever condemned the murder of a police-man or a soldier. I follow this very closely. They were always look-ing for a dove from the Sinn Féin irk. When the lord mayors made speeches in Cork they were always reported verbatim. Those Sinn Féin members had never condescended to take their seats, but they had an opportunity now to show that they were opposed to violence by accepting the prime minister's offer to meet and

dissociate themselves from these murders and outrages which alone precluded the peoples of England and Ireland, through their representatives, from making an amiable and permanent peace.[167]

In response to an MP who compared the burning of Cork City Hall and the Carnegie Free Library with the burning of Louvain by the Germans in the First World War, Greenwood declared:

There should be no comparison in fact, intention, or result. The sacking of Louvain was an attack on a whole city with great loss of life. The City Hall and the Free Library were not fired, but were burned down by the spread of the fire which the local forces and the fire brigade were unable to stop. I see a great difference between firing a building and its being burned down because of a spread of a conflagration.[168]

Greenwood then responded to the call for the cessation of burnings and shooting by saying that such acts would stop, except for 'legitimate burnings and shootings by forces of the crown. When forces were fired at from a building they were entitled to burn it down'. He then turned his attention to calls for an inquiry into government policy and declared that, 'The policy of the government and the conduct of its servants in Ireland was a matter for the House. At present Cork is under Martial Law, and no government could tolerate an inquiry by civilians into their conduct under Martial Law in an area like that'.[169] He said that all of the disorders in Ireland were 'the horrible and logical consequences of a conspiracy of extremists of the Sinn Féin movement to smash the British empire' and that the way to stop the conspiracy was to 'uproot the cause'.[170]

Greenwood welcomed what had been said in the House about Bishop Cohalan's sermon and his threat to excommunicate from the church those who attacked the forces of the crown. He said it was his belief that the overwhelming majority of Roman Catholics in Ireland desired peace and he asked the bishops and priests to undertake the collection of illegal arms. He declared he, 'couldn't imagine a more priestly or patriotic duty than the collection of such arms, for until arms illegally held are taken out of Ireland unfortunate murders would continue'.[171] In conclusion, he said he hoped that before long the response to the prime minister's speech delivered the previous Friday 'would open up a new and happier chapter of goodwill between the people of Ireland and the people of England'.[172]

T. P. O'Connor then stood up and, in an address filled with sadness, told the members that Greenwood's speech had made him think that if the prime minister was going to have any chance with his peace settlement he had better 'muzzle his chief secretary'.[173] He agreed that property was not as valuable as life but they still did not know how many lives had been lost as many people were still missing. He then referred to Greenwood's assertion that there was no evidence that the outrages in Cork had not been caused by forces of the crown and stated that he himself had read evidence of it over the past three weeks and was convinced they had been done by Black and Tans. His remarks led to cries of 'No, no!' from the government benches. When order had been restored, O'Connor continued by saying that the burnings had taken place between 9 p.m. and 2 a.m. when the Black and Tans were the only ones on the street. He then launched a direct attack on Greenwood by declaring that his policy was one of repression and that a fair, honourable and decent opportunity had been given to him to justify his statement and defend the forces of the crown at an independent inquiry but he ran off on the pretext that in time of Martial Law there could be no such inquiry. Having reminded Greenwood that an independent inquiry under a Scottish judge had been held after the Amritsar massacre, he said that the Irish should at least be treated the same as the Bengalese. O'Connor turned his attention to the chief secretary's statement that his policy had received the 'approval of the world' by asking if that was true of England and pointing out that fourteen Anglican bishops had protested against reprisals and the Archbishop of Canterbury had said that Greenwood's policy was besmirching the name of England. O'Connor finished his speech by informing the members:

I had tried to bind Irishmen in the defence of Belgium, which meant to the defence of France and England because I thought that the war would lead not only to the liberation of the small land of Belgium but to the liberation of my own small land as well. I want peace. No man in this House wants it more. I have spent forty years fighting for the liberation of Ireland and I do not want to leave this work until I see my country free, prosperous and reconciled. But the chief secretary's methods will not bring about peace. If that's what he wanted, reprisals must be stopped and the Black and Tans withdrawn. Now they were leaving bitter memories in every house. I beg the right honourable gentleman to throw away the worse half of his soul and listen to the better half – to try and stop these reprisals. What is wanted between England and Ireland is a change of heart – not merely a change of policy. In my poor way I have tried to bring about a change of heart between the two peoples but all my efforts would/will be futile if the right honourable gentleman does not put down sternly all these acts of oppression and provocation. If he did that I would wish him God-speed in every effort he made to put an end to this hideous vendetta of blood between murders and reprisals and to bring the two peoples together.[174]

On conclusion of Greenwood's remarks, the motion for adjournment was passed without a division.

Meanwhile, back in Cork, assistance had been sought from both the Limerick and Dublin Fire Brigades. Limerick duly sent a horse-drawn steamer by road while Dublin dispatched a motor pump by special train under the special supervision of chief fire officer, Captain Myers. The *Freeman's Journal* later carried an interview with Captain Myers under the heading 'Dublin Fire Chief Appalled by Destruction' which gave a graphic insight into what faced the fireman on arrival in Cork:

On being interviewed, Capt. Myers, chief of the Dublin Fire Brigade, told a *Freeman* representative that when the Dublin men arrived about 2 o'clock on Monday morning he did not think that Cork could be saved. He had worked with the men through the night. When they arrived they were in darkness, and they suddenly emerged into a sea of flames. Six streets were apparently aflame. Capt. Myers paid tribute to the manner in which the Cork firemen stood at their posts for two days, he said, 'I saw the brave boys still playing the hoses on the burning buildings. It makes me cry to see such a scene of destruction. The only way to bring it home to the people of Dublin is to say that Cork is even worse than O'Connell Street, Abbey Street and the adjoining streets after Easter Week, 1916'.[175]

A 'special correspondent' from the *Manchester Guardian* also reported:

I have no hesitation in stating that I believe all fires were incendiary fires, and that a considerable amount of petrol or some such inflammable spirit was used in one and all of them. In some cases explosives were also used, and persons were seen to go into and come out of the structures and breaking an entrance into same, and in some cases that I have attended the people have been brought out of their homes and detained in by-lanes until the fire had gained great headway. I have some of the petrol tins left behind in my possession.[176]

Then, as the citizens of Cork awoke on Monday morning, the following decree was waiting for them in both the *Cork Examiner* and *Cork Constitution* newspapers:

DECREE OF THE BISHOP OF CORK IN REFERENCE TO
AMBUSHES, KIDNAPPING AND MURDER

Besides the guilt involved in these acts by reason of their opposition to the law of God, anyone who shall, within the dioceses of Cork, organise or take part in an ambush or in kidnapping or otherwise shall be guilty of murder, or attempt at murder shall incur, by the very fact, the censure of excommunication.

DANIEL COHALAN
Bishop of Cork

Witness
PATRICK CANON SEXTON
Farranferris,
Cork.[177]

In a move clearly designed to defuse the situation General Strickland ordered K Company of the Auxiliaries to re-deploy from Victoria Barracks to Dunmanway on 13 December, where their advance party took up accommodation that evening in the town's workhouse. The problem with this was that it could also be interpreted as a disciplinary move directly related to the burning of

Cork and this was precisely how most people saw it.

However, as the week wore on, it was Greenwood's suggestion that the fires had been started by the citizens of the city themselves and that the City Hall and Carnegie Library had been set alight by fires which had spread from St Patrick's Street, that were greeted with most outrage. On Tuesday, 14 December, Dónal O'Callaghan, J. J. Walsh and Liam de Róiste sent the following telegram to Sir Hamar Greenwood, Lord R. Cecil and Messrs Asquith, Henderson, Adamson and Kenworthy:

> On behalf of the whole citizens, we absolutely and most emphatically repudiate the vile suggestion that Cork city was burned by any section of the citizens. In the name of truth, justice and civilisation, we demand an impartial inquiry into the circumstances of the city's destruction. We are quite willing to submit evidence before any international tribunal or even a tribunal of Englishmen like Bentinck, Henderson, Kenworthy and Cecil.[178]

The Cork Employer's Federation echoed the call for an inquiry that day when they adopted the following resolution:

> We, the Cork Employer's Federation, call the attention of the government to the terrible condition of things which occurred on last Saturday night and Sunday morning in Cork, by which life was lost, an enormous amount of valuable property destroyed, thousands of persons thrown out of employment, large numbers rendered homeless, and inhabitants generally kept in a state of abject terror. We demand an immediate and searching inquiry into the circumstances by an impartial tribunal. Copies of the resolution to be sent to his Excellency the Lord Lieutenant of Ireland, the Prime Minister, and the Chief Secretary of Ireland.[179]

The members of the British Labour Commission to Ireland were also incensed by Greenwood's accusations. They sent the following telegram to the British Parliamentary Labour Party which was adopted and forwarded to Lloyd George:

> The statements made by the Chief Secretary in the House of Commons confirming the burning of Cork are greatly inaccurate. The parliamentary members of the Labour Commission who visited Cork yesterday are convinced that the fires were the work of Crown Forces. The suggestion that the fire spread from Patrick Street across the river to City Hall, a distance of several hundred yards, cannot be entertained by anyone knowing the topography of Cork.
>
> We stand by our statements regarding fires in Cork, and can, if safety of witnesses is guaranteed, produce reliable evidence on the subject. We, therefore, demand independent inquiries into recent incidents in Cork. If the government refuse the British public will form its own conclusions.[180]

Incredibly, or ironically, a notice appeared in the *Times* of London that same day, signed by General Tudor, requesting more recruits for the Auxiliary Division:

> I appeal to all who have held his Majesty's commission and feel as I do – that the paramount need of the moment is the overthrow of the gang of assassins known as the Irish Republican Army – to offer themselves for service in this corps d'elite.[181]

The following day, three days after the decree of excommunication was issued by Bishop Cohalan, Father Dominic O'Connor, the chaplain to Cork No. 1 Brigade, wrote a letter to the brigade adjutant on the subject of excommunication. He said that kidnapping, ambushing and killing, ordinarily would be grave sins or violations of [church] law and, if these acts were being performed by the Volunteers as private persons (whether physical or moral) they would fall under the excommunication. However he went on to state that as the Volunteers were acting 'with the authority of the state', their acts were 'not only not sinful, but were good and meritorious' and he assured them that there was no need to worry about excommunication at all.[182]

Meanwhile, shortly after 1 p.m. that Wednesday, a group of Auxiliaries from K Company left their quarters in Dunmanway, climbed aboard two Crossley tenders and set off along the Bandon road en route for Cork city to attend the funeral of their colleague, Cadet Spencer Chapman. The officer in charge of the Auxiliaries was the district inspector who was travelling in the first lorry, while Cadet Sergeant Vernon Hart was in charge of the second. Hart was born in Lancashire on 20 November 1884 and had been a close friend of Chapman's. They had joined the Auxiliaries together in September 1920 and, after the Dillon's Cross ambush, Hart had remained at Chapman's bedside until he died. He had been very distressed since the ambush and had been selected to accompany Chapman's remains back to England. Before leaving the workhouse that morning, Hart told his fellow Auxiliaries: 'Something should be done for Chapman. I should like to see Ireland swept with fire and I should like to lead the boys'.[183]

Also out on the Bandon road that afternoon was seventy-year-old Canon Thomas J. Magner, the parish priest of Dunmanway, who had left his home near St Patrick's church at 12.30 p.m. to take his daily walk.[184] A mile or so along the way he came across a resident magistrate (RM), Mr P. Brady, who was trying to fix his car which had broken down. Brady had left Bantry earlier that morning for the military barracks in Bandon where he had official business. As he passed by, Magner exchanged a few words with him. At that moment Tadhg Crowley, a twenty-two-year-old farmer from the townland of Behigullane, and a member of Cork No. 3 Brigade of Volunteers, came along on his bicycle and the canon asked him to help Brady push the car.[185] As the men put their shoulders to the task and began to push the two Crossley tenders passed them by. A hundred yards or so up the road the second lorry stopped. Cadet Sergeant Hart jumped out, drew his revolver and stormed back towards the men. When Brady walked towards him Hart asked who he was and threatened to shoot him. Brady identified himself and Hart shoved him out of the way. He then went over to Crowley and shot him through the head before turning his attention to Canon Magner who he ordered to kneel down. Hart then fired his revolver again. When he noticed that the canon was only wounded he fired again and finished him off.

In the meantime Brady had made his way to the other Auxiliaries who, when they saw what Hart had just done, told the RM to 'clear off'. While Brady was making his escape through the fields, the first Crossley tender returned to the scene. When the district inspector saw the bodies lying on the road he ordered Hart to put his revolver back into his holster and get into the tender. He then ordered some of his men to put the bodies of Magner and Crowley on the inside of the ditch and then both vehicles returned to the workhouse. Hart was disarmed immediately on arrival and placed in the guardroom.

At around 2 p.m. Fr Michael Carmody, the senior curate in St Patrick's church, was informed that two men had been shot a mile outside the town on the Bandon road and he immediately grabbed his bicycle and went to the scene. While he was anointing the bodies another Crossley tender with a party of Auxiliaries on board arrived and the officer in charge, Major J. R. Black, expressed his regret at what had happened. The Auxiliaries then took the bodies to the mortuary in the workhouse where medical officers examined them. That evening the remains were released into the care of the local clergy and taken to St Patrick's church.

When he was informed of the deaths of Magner and Crowley, Bishop Cohalan wrote the following letter to the editor of the *Cork Examiner* which appeared in print the next morning, 16 December:

Farranferris,

December 15th, 1920

Dear Sir,

Kindly give me space to express my horror and condemnation of the terrible crime committed in Dunmanway – the murder of Canon Magner.

This is the latest move in what I call the devil's competition in crime which is taking place in our midst. I was apprehensive of some such terrible tragedy since the Kilmichael ambush. The ambush took place on the Macroom–Dunmanway road and I had reason to fear that a priest's life would be taken in reprisal. Whether that be the explanation of Canon Magner's murder or not, the ambush involved the murder of fifteen Englishmen, the deaths of three of the ambushing party, several deaths since, and it has not brought us nearer to a republic.

I offer my deepest sympathy to the relatives of Canon Magner and to the people of Dunmanway, and I take this opportunity to inform priests that the obsequies will take place on Friday in the parish church, Dunmanway.

Office and high mass at 11 o'clock.

Yours faithfully,

Daniel Cohalan[186]

When news of the incident reached General Strickland in Victoria Barracks he was outraged and immediately wrote the following letter to Bishop Cohalan:

My Lord Bishop,

I hasten to express to you the feeling of utter abhorrence and repugnance with which I heard of the murder of the Rev. Canon Thomas J. Magner, PP, last night, and the feeling is I am assured, shared by those under my command.

I wish to express to you, the members of your church, and to the family of the late Canon Magner, my deepest sympathy in the severe loss they have sustained of a priest who, I understand, was held in such high esteem by all.

I feel that I need hardly assure you that my utmost endeavours are directed towards establishing and maintaining law and order and the repression and punishment of crime of all descriptions by whomsoever they should be perpetrated.

I am, My Lord,

Yours faithfully,

E. P. Strickland

Major General Commanding 6th Division[187]

Both the adjutant and the OC of K Company joined Strickland in conveying their condolences to the bishop:

Bishop Cohalan,

The members of the Auxiliary Division, RIC, express their heartfelt sympathy to the people of Dunmanway for the loss of their revered parish priest and fellow citizen.

T. Sparrow Capt. – Adjt and D 12

For Col. Latimer, OC 'K' Coy.[188]

The Most Reverend Dr Cohalan, Lord Bishop of Cork,

Commanding Officer, Officers and Cadets of K Company, Auxiliary Division, RIC, Dunmanway, deeply regret the terrible tragedy which has deprived the parishioners and your Lordship of a priest honoured and respected by all parties and creeds. We disassociate ourselves entirely from an act which we shall never cease to regret committed by a member of the Auxiliary Division RIC.

Officer Commanding K Company

Dunmanway[189]

In Dublin Castle, the Inspector General of the RIC sent the following message to Bishop Cohalan:

Please accept my deepest sympathy on the appalling tragedy of the death of Canon Magner, and kindly convey to his relatives an express of my deep sorrow and sincere sympathy.[190]

Bishop Cohalan duly expressed his gratitude to the officers of K Company for their message of regret, but to the inspector general of the RIC he replied:

I should accept sympathy from the Inspector General of old RIC but the verbal sympathy of an Inspector General whose men are murdering my people and have burned my city, I cannot accept or convey to the relatives of murdered Canon Magner.[191]

While the people of Dunmanway struggled to come to grips with the deaths of Magner and Crowley, preparations for a military inquiry into the burning of Cork were continuing at Victoria Barracks. On 15 December, Captain Kelly sent the following notice to the editors of the local newspapers who printed it the following morning:

Major General Sir E. P. Strickland, K.C.B., M.C., D.S.O., Commanding 6th Division directs me to inform you that an inquiry will be held at these headquarters on Saturday, December 18th, in connection with the burning and looting of property in Cork City on the night of 11th/12th inst.

All persons willing to give evidence in this case and in a position to do so are requested to communicate with these headquarters as soon as possible.

Names of witnesses will not be published in the press.

C. J. O'C. Kelly. Captain

Attached General Staff 6th Division

Headquarters, 6th Division, Cork. 15.12.20.[192]

Not surprisingly, the civic authorities immediately refused to participate. When Strickland sent a telegram to the city engineer asking him to appear before the military inquiry he received the following reply from Cork Corporation:

We have instructed the city engineer and other corporate officials to take no part in the English military inquiry into the burning of this city, with which we charge the English military and police forces before the whole world. We adhere to the offer made by the city members and the lord mayor to submit evidence already in our possession before an impartial military tribunal, or before a court of fair-minded Englishmen.[193]

Other bodies were quite willing to participate but when Maurice Healy, a solicitor and ex-MP for Cork, wrote to General Strickland on 16 December offering to give evidence on behalf of the Cork Chamber of Commerce and the Cork Employers' Federation, he was informed that lawyers would not be admitted to the inquiry.

In a House of Commons debate that same evening the issue of how the fires on St Patrick's Street had managed to 'spread' to City Hall was finally addressed when Captain Redmond asked the chief secretary:

> in view of what has taken place in West Cork and owing to the
> opportunity that has since been afforded him of studying the topo-
> graphy of Cork City, does the right honourable gentleman still
> adhere to the suggestion that the flames spread from Patrick Street
> over an intervening area which has been untouched, including the
> river, to the City Hall?[194]

In response, Greenwood admitted that:

> the remarks I made in reference to the spread of the flames were
> given to me in reports I had received and in those reports coming
> to me the conflagration was understood to be larger and more wide-
> spread than it turned out to be. If I was in error, I unreservedly
> withdraw.[195]

While this debate continued in London the inaugural meeting of
a relief fund committee was being held in the council chamber at
Cork courthouse. Professor O'Rahilly, TC, was chairman and in
attendance were: Alderman Denis Lucy, Simon O'Mahony, TC;
Alderman Liam de Róiste; W. J. Fahy, secretary of the Farmers'
Union; B. Haughton, HC; S. H. Newman, HC; T. Coyle and
M. Hill of the TGWU; Seán O'Leary, TC; John French, TC;
Michael Ó'Cuill, TC; and George Nason, president of the Cork
and Districts Trades Council.

Professor O'Rahilly proposed that the principal order of business
be the issuing of an interim appeal. Liam de Róiste then classified
those requiring relief under three headings: those who were very
poor and who should be immediately relieved; those who were unemployed but were perhaps not needy; and those whose property
and premises had been destroyed. It was unanimously agreed that

the lord mayor be authorised to deal with urgent cases from funds already donated by William O'Brien and Mr Mackesy. It was then agreed that an interim appeal should be made for funds and that subscriptions would be received either by the lord mayor or the local banks.

A letter was then read from the secretary of the Draper's Assistants Association stating that over 400 of their members had lost their employment and requesting that two of their members be co-opted on to the committee. After this was agreed de Róiste mentioned that he had received a cable from America stating that supplies of food were being sent to Ireland immediately but he had cabled back that plenty of food was available in Ireland if the necessary funds were forthcoming. When the committee expressed its approval for de Róiste's action he replied by declaring that 'there were sufficient Cork people in America to rebuild the whole city'.[196] He then moved a vote of thanks to William O'Brien for his generosity which was approved and the meeting adjourned for a week.

In London that day, the Labour Commission of Inquiry, which had returned from Ireland, attended a joint meeting of the National Executive and the Parliamentary Labour Party to report the result of its investigations. During the meeting, the members read out a statement in which they revealed the extent of their inquiries into the burning of Cork. They reported that 'the news of the destruction in Cork did not come as a surprise to the commission' and that during its stay in Cork they 'could not avoid the feeling that a serious outbreak of trouble was probable'. In the wake of the burning of the city, two members had returned to visit the affected areas and had taken evidence from a number of 'responsible citizens'. Businessmen had informed them that the cost of the damage might run into millions of pounds and that:

the disaster will involve the unemployment of a considerable number of workers in addition to those who will be indirectly thrown out of work as a result of the fire [and] the commerce of the city has already suffered very appreciably as a result of the events of recent months, and the incendiarism of the past weekend will strike a further blow at the economic activities of the city of Cork.[197]

Having outlined the events of the night of 11/12 December the statement said that, 'the members of the commission made special inquiries regarding the origin and cause of the fires and numerous witnesses were interviewed. They were unanimous in stating that the fires had been caused by the crown forces'. The commissioners then concluded by saying that they had failed to obtain an interview with the military to get official information on the Dillon's Cross ambush and the subsequent fires. The outcome of the meeting was a decision to urge the prime minister to make a further effort to bring about a truce in Ireland with a view to negotiations being held between representatives of the government and the elected representatives of the Irish people.

By now, an escort of Auxiliaries had removed Cadet Sergeant Hart from his cell in Dunmanway Workhouse and returned him to Cork where he was incarcerated in the Military Detention Barracks to await his fate. In the afternoon, a military inquiry (not an inquest) was held in the RIC barracks in Dunmanway and a number of Auxiliaries testified that Hart had indeed shot both Canon Magner and Tadhg Crowley. One witness described Hart as having been drinking steadily for some time while another declared he was 'as mad as a hatter'.[198] Resident Magistrate Brady also testified, as did two doctors who gave evidence as to the wounds suffered by both men and the cause of their deaths.

Next morning, Friday, 17 December, the town of Dunmanway closed down for the concelebrated funeral mass which took place at 11 a.m. in St Patrick's church. Bishop Cohalan presided and

116 priests from the dioceses of Cork, Cloyne, Ross and Kerry were present. After mass, the remains of both men were laid to rest in the church grounds.

That same day, with the conduct of the crown forces now under intense scrutiny, General Macready wrote the following order which was clearly designed to curb excessive use of force:

MARTIAL LAW CIRCULAR NO. 1

Full powers have been given me as General Officer Commanding-in-Chief to restore order in those counties in Ireland where Martial Law has been proclaimed and all forces of the Crown may rest assured that as long as these forces in their actions to restore order do not exceed what is reasonably necessary for the purpose they will have my full approval and support; but all forces of the Crown are hereby warned against commission of the following offences, namely -

(1) Committing an offence against the person or property of an inhabitant of, or resident in, this country, or

(2) Breaking into any house or other place in search of plunder, or

(3) Forcing a sentry on duty for the protection of some person or property.

(4) Forcing or striking a soldier when acting as a sentinel.
    Any person subject to military or Martial Law who has committed any of the above offences will, on conviction by a court-martial or military court, be liable to suffer death.[199]

Twenty-four hours later, on 18 December, Con Delany finally lost his fight for life when he died from his wounds in the Mercy Hospital. While the Delany family were busy making funeral arrangements that Saturday, General Strickland's military inquiry into the burning of Cork opened at Victoria Barracks. The court consisted of Lieutenant Colonel Stapleton, Major Parker and Major Kerns, with Major Milton employed as legal officer. Milton was tasked with interrogating the witnesses, who were drawn from the army, the Auxiliaries and the RIC.

Meanwhile, at Farranferris, appalled at what he now perceived as a downward spiral of violence, and responding to criticism levelled at him by the Corporation, Bishop Cohalan decided to write a pastoral letter which would be read at all masses on Sunday, 19 December. He began by declaring that Cork had been free of the 'crime of murder' until the previous March and he went on to relate the facts, as he knew them, surrounding the deaths of Constable Murtagh and Tomás MacCurtain. He then posed the question:

> what has the country gained politically by the murder of police-men and by the burning of barracks and of historical or costly buildings? Some republicans used to speak of the receding autho-rity of England and of the occupation of deserted districts by the advancing authority of the republic when some policemen were murdered and their barracks burned. He would be a bold republican who would talk now in a city or county of districts delivered from British rule. No – the killing of policemen was morally murder and politically of no consequence, and the burning of barracks was simply the destruction of Irish property.[200]

Cohalan went on to examine the ambushes at Kilmichael and Dillon's Cross:

> The ambushers came from nobody knows where, and when they have done their work disappear – nobody knows to what destination. Ordinarily, there is very little risk to the ambushers themselves as there is no risk in shooting a policeman from behind

a screen. But by this time boys and men taking part in ambushes must know that by their criminal act they are exposing perhaps a whole countryside, perhaps a town or city, to the danger of terrible reprisals.[201]

He then addressed what he called the 'crimes of individuals and government crimes' and stated that:

the crimes of the government in Ireland are on a different plane, and are infinitely greater than the crimes of a private military organisation because it is the duty of the government, through its servants to protect the lives and property of the citizens, especially innocent, unoffending citizens. But instead of defending the lives and property of the innocent, the government, by a carefully laid plan, for which not even a cloak of legality has been provided, has conducted through its servants a reprisal campaign of murder of the innocent and of the destruction of their property.[202]

In conclusion, Bishop Cohalan was unambiguously clear where he stood on the subject of 'murder and excommunication':

the killing of an individual is murder, and ambushes are murderous. Some complain if in the same discourse I condemn the murder of a policeman and of a civilian; others complain if, when condemning murder, I condemn bad government, coercion and reprisals. But murder is murder, and arson is arson, whether committed by agents of the government or by members of the Republican Army, and it is the duty of a bishop to denounce murder and arson, from whatever source they come. In the awful circumstances in which we live, to protect our men and boys from the danger of murder and arson, and to protect the community at large from the evil of reprisals, I notify again to the faithful of the dioceses, through the different churches, the decree of excommunication, which has already been promulgated and is in force.[203]

But nobody was listening to the bishop. When he read the letter himself at noon mass in the North Cathedral some members of the congregation walked out. Later that afternoon Liam de Róiste's house in Sunday's Well was raided by the military and the Sinn Féin MP for Cork was arrested and taken to Victoria Barracks. There he was asked if he had any evidence to give to the Strickland inquiry but when he stated that he had not, he was released.

In the meantime, Maurice Healy was still trying to establish why he had been refused permission to appear before the inquiry. He had written to Strickland on both 17 and 21 December only to be informed: 'As the court of inquiry has now closed, your question does not arise'. This confirmed the belief held by virtually all the citizens of Cork that any inquiry held by the military 'would be closed before it was opened' and consequently a complete waste of time.

Of far greater importance to the citizens of Cork was the on-going effort to generate funds to alleviate the hardship caused by the burnings. On 21 December the *Cork Examiner* carried the following appeal from the lord mayor:

APPEAL FOR FUNDS

The citizens of Cork regret that it is necessary for them to make a public and universal appeal for funds to enable them to deal with the widespread distress and unemployment caused not only by the recent burning of the city, involving direct damage of about three million pounds and enormous consequential damages, but also by the previous economic conditions, murders and arson, of which this last great conflagration is but the culminating tragedy.

With the heart of our city in ruins, our municipal buildings, our public library and numerous houses completely burnt to the ground, with our finest shops looted, with our industries crippled, our own resources are insufficient to provide food, clothing, work and homes for those in want.

We, therefore, confidently appeal for immediate help to all those, without distinction of race, creed or class, who are able and willing to lessen suffering in our stricken city.

We expect and request the employers in the city to keep all their present staffs employed, and under no circumstances to create any further unemployment.

Dómnall Ua Ceallacáin,
Lord Mayor of Cork.

Later that evening Cadet Sergeant Hart was brought before a general court-martial in Victoria Barracks and charged with the murder of Magner and Crowley. After the charges were read, counsel for the defence, James Rearden, BL, said more time was required to allow a medical officer to establish whether Hart was in a fit mental condition to enter a plea. The president of the court adjourned proceedings until 5 January 1921.

None of this mattered to the ordinary people of Cork who were now facing into a Christmas filled with uncertainty. With their city in ruins and the misery of long-term unemployment already affecting hundreds of families, the future for most people looked very dark indeed.

Undaunted, Cork No. 1 Brigade decided to continue military operations and finish the year as they had started it. On Friday, 24 December, in a move designed to silence the *Cork Examiner* because of its perceived pro-government position, Volunteers raided its offices on St Patrick's Street and damaged the printing presses. Then, four days after Christmas, they demonstrated how proficient they had become in the art of guerrilla warfare when members of the 4th Battalion, Cork No. 1 Brigade, mounted an operation against the RIC in the town of Midleton. At 9.45 p.m. a ten-man RIC foot patrol was advancing down both sides of the Main Street when it was attacked by the Volunteers who opened fire from three directions. Constable Martin Mullin was shot dead and five other constables were seriously wounded.[204] The remaining members of the patrol managed to return safely to their barracks and the district inspector sent to Cork for reinforcements. An RIC detachment of four lorries, accompanied by two ambulances, was immediately dispatched from the city. When the convoy was a mile and a half outside Midleton, near Glebe House, it too was ambushed by a squad of Volunteers who had blocked the road with a felled tree. Two members of the RIC, Sergeant Nolan and Constable Poddy, were wounded in this engagement and the Volunteers managed to escape unharmed.

The British authorities were swift to respond. On New Year's Eve night, a large party of soldiers and policemen surrounded the Cork Union Workhouse and conducted a thorough search of the premises in an effort to see if any Volunteers were hiding there. All the inmates were rounded up, put into one location and placed under armed guard while they waited to be searched and questioned by an army doctor. Staff members were also detained and questioned by military and police officers. As the operation involved a considerable number of troops and was expected to take quite a while, a field kitchen was actually brought from Victoria Barracks to provide hot food for those engaged in the operation which lasted until 2.30 p.m. on New Year's Day.

The first day of 1921 saw the conflict enter a new phase when the first 'official' British military reprisal operation occurred. In the immediate aftermath of the Midleton and Glebe House attacks an air of fear and trepidation descended upon the people of the locality as they awaited the reaction of the crown forces. This came shortly after 3 p.m. on Saturday 1 January when a number of lorries containing soldiers and policemen descended upon Midleton. People walking in the streets were detained and subjected to a thorough search after which they were ordered to go back to their homes and pull down the blinds. The military then proceeded to three houses on Main Street: the homes of John O'Shea, the chairman of the Midleton Board of Guardians; Edward Carey, chairman of the Midleton Urban Council; and Paul McCarthy. The inhabitants of these houses were then given a copy of a document entitled 'Notice B' which read as follows:

> WHEREAS attacks by unknown rebels were made on the Forces of the Crown on the 29th December at MIDLETON and near GLEBE HOUSE, MIDLETON, in the County of Cork, and whereas it is considered that you being in the vicinity of the outrages were bound to have known of the ambushes and attacks and that you neglected to give any information to the military or police authorities, now therefore I, Brigadier General H. W. Higginson, C.B., D.S.O., Commanding 17th Infantry Brigade and Military Governor have ordered the destruction of your property.
> Signed in Cork this first day of January 1921.
>
> H. W. Higginson
Brigadier General
Military Governor[205]

Having been served with this notice, the inhabitants were given one hour to collect their valuables – with the exception of furniture – and evacuate their homes. Once that was complete, the soldiers moved in and destroyed the buildings using explosives. The crown forces then left for the vicinity of Glebe House where they served another 'Notice B' on the Cotter and Donovan homes in Ballyadam, and the Dorgan and Ahern homes at Knockgriffin. These were also destroyed.

In the meantime, Strickland's military inquiry into the burning of Cork had been completed. Only one copy of the report was made and this document was sent to London on 30 December. On 4 January, it was placed before a special meeting of the British cabinet.

In Cork the following day the trial of Cadet Sergeant Hart resumed in Victoria Barracks. Medical witnesses stated that in their opinion Hart was now capable of following the evidence and understood the gravity of the charges placed against him. During the proceedings, RM Brady gave evidence against Hart and he was followed by some of the Auxiliaries who had witnessed the shootings. A number of medical witnesses were then called to give evidence as to the state of Hart's mind on 15 December 1920. When the trial concluded at 7.30 p.m. the findings of the court were that:

> In the case of Temporary Cadet Sergeant Vernon Hart, RIC, charged before a general court-martial at Cork on Wednesday 5th January 1921, with the murder of Very Reverend Canon Magner, PP, and Mr Tadhg Crowley, near Dunmanway on 15th December 1920, the court found that the accused was guilty of the offences with which he was charged, but was insane at the time of their commission. The finding has been confirmed and promulgated.[206]

Two days previously, on 3 January 1921, Major Bernard Law Montgomery had arrived in Cork to take up the appointment of Brigade Major of 17th Infantry Brigade. Morale was low discipline was weak, and relations with the RIC, the Black and Tans, and the Auxiliaries had reached an all time low. The civilian population had come to deeply resent the British administration following their failure to prevent the sacking of the city, and the Volunteers remained intact, invisible and secure as they planned their next offensive operations. This was a critical time, capable of either developing into outright warfare or smouldering along in a fraught and uneasy co-existence. In an effort to improve the situation, Montgomery began drafting a series of instructions which he believed were necessary to increase the efficiency of the 17th Brigade and to regain the support of the civilian population.[207] But this initiative came too late. By now the citizens of Cork had lost all confidence in the forces of law and order, and to make matters worse, on 19 January the British cabinet decided to suppress the Strickland Report.

11

WHO BURNED CORK?

As a result of the British government's decision to suppress the findings of Strickland's inquiry into the burning of the city, several significant questions remained unanswered. For example, there was still no official answer to the simple question of who had burned Cork. As far as the majority of Cork citizens were concerned there was never any doubt who was responsible for burning their city. Virtually the entire population believed it had been primarily the work of members of K Company of the Auxiliary Division of the RIC stationed in Victoria Barracks. Upon their return to Britain, the British Labour Party commission issued a statement in which they said:

> The members of the Commission made special inquiries into the origins and cause of the fires and numerous witnesses were interviewed. They were unanimous in stating that the fires were caused by Crown Forces.[208]

It was also well known within the British military establishment who bore responsibility for the deed. General Macready later wrote of the Strickland inquiry:

> An inquiry was immediately held, as a result of which there was no doubt that the fires and subsequent looting were the work of a company of the Auxiliary Division of the police who had

recently arrived in Cork, and who had been exasperated by a rebel ambush at a place called Dillon's Cross. No lives were lost, though some shooting took place between the Auxiliaries and rebels in the streets.[209]

Macready was critical of the decision to suppress the findings:

> For some reason which I have never discovered, the Castle authorities decided not to make public the opinion of the inquiry on the burnings in Cork, a mistaken policy in my opinion, since it gave greater scope to the rebel propaganda, and it was no secret in the town as to who were the culprits. The proper course, to my mind, would have been to mete out exemplary punishment to the responsible officers, and to any men who could be identified as having been actual participators in the affair; instead of which those responsible for the administration of the forces talked of disbanding the whole division.[210]

General Tudor held his own RIC inquiry into what had happened that night but, not surprisingly, his findings were somewhat different to those of the military. District Inspector Deignan, who was the RIC representative on Strickland's inquiry, complained that neither the questions he had addressed to witnesses nor the answers he received were actually recorded. He also attempted to shift some of the responsibility for the burning to the military when he stated:

> I understand there were 2,433 soldiers in Cork on the night of 11th December, this appears ample force to have prevented Cork being burnt. It does not appear to have been used. My opinion is that K Company could not possibly have been in a position to pick out particular houses to burn as they had only been a few days in

Cork. Colonel Latimer seems to have done his best to control and account for his men. I think it is possible that some odd members of K Company were implicated in the burnings; there is no proof as to individuals, and therefore, legally, it is impossible to bring the charges home. There is no evidence to show that more than one soldier was implicated, and he was a soldier in kilts. In my opinion, people are not likely to give evidence against soldiers before a military tribunal.[211]

Colonel Latimer also dismissed the findings of the military inquiry stating that, 'A military court judging a matter of that kind is bound to be unconsciously prejudiced' and that the military authorities had refused to summons the civilian witnesses he had asked to be called. He further stated that:

The case was already prejudged by the action of the military authorities in clearing the police off the streets at 3 a.m.; it was then that the looting began. It was also prejudiced by sending K Company out of Cork the next day.[212]

Latimer went on to testify, somewhat incredulously, that far from being responsible for the fires, his men had actually helped to bring the conflagration under control:

I got the gas turned off at 3 a.m. as this seemed a reason for the fire spreading. I did this by telephoning the gas authorities, but they objected as I was not the C.M.A. [Competent Military Authority] I had to use threats to get the gas turned off ... The whole 55 men of my party were working in sections under my supervision till 3 a.m. when I sent the majority of them back to barracks as the police were ordered off the streets by the military authorities.

My men did not know their way about the streets and they could not have sufficient knowledge to have burnt the houses if chosen. The Cork Savings Bank and another bank near the Mall were guarded by my patrols. Fires had been occurring in Cork 10 days previous to the arrival of K Company.[213]

Despite the evidence given by the RIC and Auxiliaries, when General Tudor sent his report to the chief secretary he felt the need to add a note in his own handwriting which stated that 'I have not been able to disprove that some members of K Co. were implicated'.[214]

General Crozier, the officer commanding the Auxiliary Division, later expressed his contempt for the inquiry held by the RIC:

In order to offset the Strickland report the police hierarchy held an inquiry of their own which helped the government considerably, not that it was any more 'reliable' than the military document, but because the new bias and 'inaccuracy' came from the right quarter, and carried with it a sweeter aroma. A 'Tannery' does not as a rule produce the nicest of smells.

The most reliable document in existence dealing with the Cork fires is the report of the Irish Labour Party and Trade Union Congress … which sets out freely the attitude of hypocrisy and duplicity of the government, the futility and unreliability of the military inquiry and the reign of chaos, murder, arson, robbery and drunkenness which General Strickland seemed able to tolerate without himself going mad.[215]

Crozier also condemned the attempts made by Hamar Greenwood in the House of Commons to blame the destruction of the City Hall and Carnegie Library on flames which 'spread' from St

Patrick's Street and to suggest that the citizens of Cork were responsible for burning their own city:

> It takes a clever man to be a good liar. The first 'slip' came when a politician in a responsible position in answer to a question by an Irishman in the House of Commons, one who knew Cork (the man in authority did not) stated that the fires had 'spread' from Patrick Street to the City Hall. The element of surprise had been used in the House of Commons on this subtle and cunning politician with the result that, knowing nothing about what he was talking and being far away from his propaganda department, he behaved – well – foolishly, to say the least of it, for the south channel of the River Lee, about a hundred yards wide, intervened between the City Hall and Patrick Street, while the nearest blaze was some five hundred yards distant from the City Hall, and the wind was not blowing from north-west to south-east which was the only condition which could have possibly blown a spark five hundred yards across a wide river to a masonry-built building and set fire to it; and even the suggestion was ridiculous.
>
> To bolster this ridiculous contention that the City Hall had been burned by fires 'spreading' a faked map was published in a London newspaper showing the City Hall to be where it is not, namely to the north of and adjacent to Patrick Street! In those days the press (with the honourable exception of the *Manchester Guardian*, *Daily News* and *Westminster Gazette*) went hand in glove with the official propaganda department to help keep Lloyd George in power.
>
> The moment the diabolical lie that the Irish had burnt their city was uttered, protests from the city of Cork were received by the more fair-minded, and therefore more honourably equipped, Englishmen – including Mr Asquith and Lord Robert Cecil – asking for an impartial and judicial inquiry.[216]

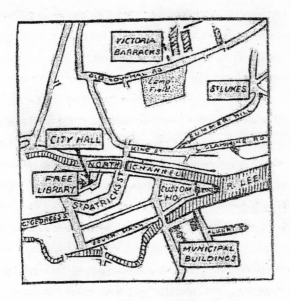

Map from Who Burnt Cork city, originally published in *The Daily Chronicle* on
13 December 1920

Crozier also took issue with the findings of what he labelled the
'Strickland Farce':

> The report condemned the police while whitewashing the soldiers
> and censured General Tudor [the chief of police] for sending a
> 'new and hastily raised company' to Cork. I sent the company to
> Cork and not General Tudor, and if any blame was attachable I
> should have received it despite the fact that I was in hospital ... It
> was a most unfair accusation to have ever levelled against General
> Tudor, an accusation supported by the man who had convened the
> court and by his own neglect had allowed the burning and sacking
> of Cork to take place.[217]

The main documentary evidence connecting K Company to the
burning of the city was found in two letters intercepted by the

Volunteers. Shortly after arrival in Dunmanway an Auxiliary cadet who signed himself as 'Charlie' wrote to his mother stating that he was 'recovering from a chill contracted on Saturday night during the burning of Cork'. He went on to state that:

> We did it all night. Never mind how much the well intentioned Hamar Greenwood would excuse us. In all my life and in all the tales of fiction I have read, I have never experienced such orgies of murder, arson and looting as I have witnessed the past 16 days.[218]

In a second letter, addressed to 'Edith', he wrote:

> We are having a h___ of a time here. You will have read all about Cork. Suffice to say I was there and very actively employed to boot until the dawn on Sunday. I just escaped the ambush in which 8 of our boys were wounded but arrived later as a reinforcement. We took a sweet revenge.[219]

Taking all of this evidence together, it becomes clear that a variety of military and police commanders all had serious questions to answer in relation to the activity of personnel under their respective commands. It is also clear that General Strickland had a case to answer in his own right because personnel under his command carried out the burning. The city of Cork was in Strickland's area of operations. It was also under Martial Law – and under Martial Law the police forces operating in the city (including the Auxiliaries) were subordinate to the military commander. Strickland was the military commander and in that capacity was well aware of the Dillon's Cross ambush and the events which took place there in the aftermath. Yet he took no action to stop retaliation administered against property in the immediate vicinity. It is equally clear that he also took no action to halt the arson attacks and looting in the city centre when they got underway, nor did he provide military assistance to the fire brigade to combat the fires when requested to do so. His failure to take action in relation to any of these matters leaves him culpable and in dereliction of his duty.

When parliament resumed on 15 February several speakers questioned the Prime Minister, Lloyd George, on the Strickland Report. He replied by stating that the report indicated there had been acts of indiscipline on the part of some members of the Auxillary forces. Seven personnel had been suspected of indiscipline and dismissed. The commanding officer had been suspended and the company had been dissolved with the members reassigned. However the report itself remained under lock and key.[220]

12

CONCLUSIONS

The burning of Cork city on the night of 11/12 December 1920 was the single largest reprisal conducted by crown forces in Ireland during the War of Independence. In order to explain why it happened one must look again at the sequence of events which preceded it and place them in a context where the burning of buildings in reprisal for Volunteer violence was already commonplace.

As previously identified, the strategy adopted by the Volunteers during the first year of the War of Independence consisted for the most part of isolated attacks on members of the RIC. This led to large numbers of resignations from the force which increased further as the Volunteer campaign intensified. The British government's response to this upsurge in violence was two fold: the introduction of new police reinforcements, and the appointments of Sir Hamar Greenwood as chief secretary, General Sir Nevil Macready as commander-in-chief, and General Hugh Tudor as police advisor.

Despite the steady increase in Volunteer activity the British government still considered them to be nothing more than a bunch of murderers and criminals who should be dealt with, in the first instance by the RIC with the British army acting in support. But the RIC were now becoming extremely vulnerable and isolated themselves. Outraged by attacks on individual constables and several police barracks, and frustrated by the fact that the Volunteers could operate freely by hiding within the civilian population, some members of the force in Cork felt that the time had come to take retaliatory action against leading members of the republican movement. A secret meeting was held in the city early in 1920 to discuss this matter and, while the majority present eventually voted against targeting individual republicans, a minority trenchantly held the view that this might be a very useful tactic because they believed reprisals were the only effective way to strike fear into the hearts of their opponents.[221]

With violence continuing, and pressure on the RIC intensifying, the government passed the Restoration of Order in Ireland Act on 9 August 1920 which gave sweeping new powers to the forces of the crown. The *Weekly Summary*, which first appeared on 13 August 1920, also served as an incitement to violence. The issue published on the 10 December 1920, the day before the burning of Cork, compared the Kilmichael ambush to Turkish atrocities and described the Volunteers as 'fiends and not men'.

Opinion had also hardened within Cork No. 1 Brigade at this time and the meeting of Florrie O'Donoghue and Josephine Brown in September 1920 enabled the Volunteers to embark on a campaign to eliminate the network of British spies and informers that was operating in Cork city. This increased tension even further.

Unable to win the war because this was not a conventional conflict, some elements within the forces of law and order then adopted unconventional means and arson became a preferred tactic when reprisals were considered necessary. In this context the burning of Cork started long before the night of 11/12 December 1920 and may in fact be traced to the evening of 27 September when the premises of Castle and Co. were set ablaze probably in direct retaliation for the Volunteers' abduction of Seán O'Callaghan twelve days earlier.

The following month saw the arrival of the first members of the Auxiliary force in Cork and this coincided with a marked increase in the number of arson attacks made in the city together with the first mention in the newspapers of the shadowy 'Anti-Sinn Fein Society'. As the arson attacks continued the perpetrators were no doubt encouraged by the refusal of the British government to initiate an inquiry into events in Cork – despite repeated calls from the opposition benches to do so. The perpetrators could also draw encouragement from the memorandum issued by General Tudor on 12 November in which he said 'The RIC will have the fullest support in the most drastic action against the band of assassins, the so-called IRA.'[222]

However, for all their attempts at coercion, either by direct arson attacks or the issuance of threats in the newspapers by the Anti-Sinn Féin Society, neither the will of the Volunteers nor the population at large was affected. As far as the Volunteers were concerned, their campaign was working and they would not be deflected. From the perspective of those members of the crown forces engaged in unofficial reprisals, their security had now been breached, no action was having the desired effect, and a bad situation was simply getting worse.

In this context, a major deterioration in morale took place immediately after the Kilmichael ambush with the realisation that a major defeat had been inflicted upon the Auxiliaries. Morale plummeted further when the newspapers carried the report of Dr Kelleher's findings in relation to the condition of the bodies. And finally, when a patrol was attacked at Dillon's Cross it became clear that the crown forces were no longer safe anywhere, even if they travelled in large numbers. Considering all these factors and the timeframe involved, it was inevitable that a reprisal on a grand scale would take place.

Writing subsequently about the burning of Cork, Florrie O'Donoghue stated:

It is difficult to say with certainty whether or not Cork would have been burned on that night if there had not been an ambush [at

Dillon's Cross]. What appears more probable is that the ambush provided the excuse for an act which was long premeditated and for which all arrangements had been made. The rapidity with which the supplies of petrol and Verey lights were brought from Cork barracks to the centre of the city, and the deliberate manner in which the work of firing the premises was divided amongst groups under the control of officers, gives evidence of organisation and pre-arrangement. Moreover, the selection of certain premises for destruction, and the attempt made by an Auxiliary officer to prevent the looting of one shop by Black and Tans [when he said]: 'You are in the wrong shop; that man is a loyalist,' and the reply, 'We don't give a damn; this is the shop that was pointed out to us', is additional proof that the matter had been carefully planned beforehand.[223]

O'Donoghue's assessment is correct. The evidence suggests that the burning of the city was planned by elements within the RIC long before the night of 11/12 December 1920 – possibly a short time after the Kilmichael ambush – and that the Dillon's Cross ambush was simply the spark which ignited the flame. The forces of law and order had reached the point of no return when the decision was taken to burn the city of Cork. This was their attempt to regain control – and it failed miserably. Instead five acres of property were destroyed, the damage was assessed at several million pounds and around 2,000 people were put out of work.

For many years afterwards the Volunteers who mounted the Dillon's Cross ambush firmly believed they had been directly responsible for the burning of Cork and the murder of the two Delany brothers. Some of them even carried this burden of guilt all the way to their graves. However the evidence suggests that while the attack at Dillon's Cross was significant, on its own it would not have triggered the response which subsequently unfolded. A better explanation places the events at Dillon's Cross in an evolving sequence of Volunteer violence which in turn generated a massive reprisal designed to strike at the Volunteers by punishing those who harboured them.

The burning of Cork was a defining moment in the War of Independence. It galvanised the Volunteers and the people of the city for the trials which lay ahead. It also confirmed the truth of the words spoken by Terence MacSwiney on his inauguration as lord mayor, when he said: 'It is not they who can inflict the most, but they who can suffer the most, will conquer'.

APPENDIX 1

**Memorandum concerning discipline within the RIC issued by
General Tudor on 12 November 1920**

D 446

1920

RI Constabulary Office

Dublin Castle

12 November 1920

Discipline

The following memorandum is transmitted for the information and
guidance of officers and men of the Royal Irish Constabulary.

C. A. Walsh

Deputy Inspector General

The Royal Irish Constabulary has shown unparalleled fortitude in
standing up to a diabolical murder campaign. Discipline has been
maintained at a very high level. To ensure uniformity of action and of
discipline the following directions are issued for guidance. The RIC
will have the fullest support in the most drastic action against the
band of assassins, the so-called IRA. These murderers must be pursued
relentlessly and their organisation ruthlessly suppressed. The initiative
must be seized, the ambushers must be ambushed. The leaders and
members of the criminal gang are mostly known to us. They must be
given no rest. They must be hunted down. But, for the effectual performance of these duties, the highest discipline is essential. There must
be no wild firing from lorries. It is useless and dangerous to innocent

people. Firearms should never be fired except with the intention of hitting the object aimed at. Firing in the air or over the heads of crowds is strictly forbidden. It is dangerous to innocent people in the far distance. Property must be respected or women and children and innocent people will suffer; there must be no arson or looting. The Officers, Head Constables and Sergeants must see to this. I look to them to enforce discipline. The police exist to restore and maintain order in Ireland. They must show forbearance and preserve their discipline, whatever the provocation. Women must invariably be respected. Because the cowardly blackguards of the IRA cut woman's hair, it is no reason why the RIC should retaliate by similar action. Such conduct cannot and will not be tolerated. The police grow strong every day. Decent men who have been deluded or forced into joining the IRA are resigning. By continuing their firm and resolute pressure against this criminal organisation, the police will lift the terror from the people of Ireland.

H. H. Tudor, Major General
Police Advisor.

APPENDIX 2

Memorandum concerning reprisals by members of the RIC, issued by General Tudor on 6 December 1920

D 466

1920

Royal Irish Constabulary Office

Dublin Castle

6 December 1920

Burning of Houses, Etc.

The following copy of a memorandum issued by the Police Advisor is sent for the information and guidance of officers and men of the RI Constabulary.

C. A. Walsh

Deputy Inspector General

Copy

Office of the Police Advisor

Dublin Castle

There have been recently a large number of reports of arson. Whilst by no means clear that this is done by the Forces of the Crown, I wish again to impress on all members of the Police Force the absolute necessity of stopping burnings whatever the provocation. The only justifiable burnings are the destruction of buildings from which fire is opened on Forces of the Crown. Burnings of houses or buildings not directly connected with assassination or attempted assassination, is indefensible. I appeal to the police of all ranks to suppress all destruction of property in Ireland even of notorious Sinn Féiners. The Force will now fully recognise that the Government is giving them full support and I feel sure that they do not wish to embarrass the Government in their very difficult task of exterminating the murder organisation. I can assure them that the incendiarism tends to alienate the sympathy of many right thinking and law abiding citizens of the Empire and does harm to the cause of right for which we are fighting.

H. H. Tudor, Major General
Police Advisor

(issued to all DCs, CIs, Dis and all existing stations)

APPENDIX 3

**The Official Report of the Superintendent of the City of Cork Fire
Brigade into the Burning of Cork**

15 December 1920

The Right Hon. The Lord Mayor of Cork.

Sir,

In reference to the fires which occurred in the city on Saturday night,
December 11, 1920, I beg to report as follows:

At 10.30 p.m. I received a call to Messrs. A. Grant and Co., Patrick
Street, whose extensive premises were on fire. I found that the fire had
gained considerable headway and the flames were coming through the
roof. I got three lines of hose to work – one in Mutton Lane and two
in Market lane, intersecting passages on either side of the premises.
With a good supply of water we were successful in confining the fire
to Messrs. Grant's, Patrick Street premises, and prevented its spread to
that portion running to the Grand Parade from Mutton Lane, which
we saved, except with slight damage, the adjacent premises of Messrs.
Hackett (jeweller) and Haynes (jeweller). The Market – a building
mostly of timber – to the rear of Messrs. Grants was found to be in
great danger. If this building became involved a conflagration would
ensue with which it would be almost impossible to cope. Except for
only a few minor outbreaks in the roof we were successful in saving
the Market and also other valuable premises in Mutton Lane.

During the above operations I received word from the Town Clerk
that the Munster Arcade was on fire. This was about 11.30 p.m. I sent
all the men and appliances available to contend with it. Shortly after I
got word that Messrs. Cash's premises were on fire. I shortened down

hose at Mutton Lane and sent all available stand-pipes, hose &c., and men to contend with this fire. I found both the Munster Arcade and Messrs. Cash's were alight from end to end, with no prospect of saving either, and the fire spreading rapidly to the adjoining property. The area involved in these two fires was very large and embraced many valuable and extensive premises.

All the hydrants and mains that we could possibly use were brought to bear upon the flames and points were selected were the fore may be possibly checked and our efforts concentrated there. The General Post Office fire appliances were brought out and did good service in and around Winthrop Street, Robert Street, &c. I regret to state that I found this new hose cut in several places whilst in the streets and was of no further use. It was not until about 8 a.m. when I may state that the whole of the numerous points to which the flames had reached were partially under control.

About 4 a.m. I was informed that the Municipal Buildings were on fire. Knowing that there was a practical man with half a dozen men under his control there I had some confidence that they would be able to deal effectively with the fire as had already been done on previous occasions. I very much regret, however, that the incendiaries were successful in driving my men out of the buildings and also from the Carnagie Free Library.

I continued to do my best to confine the fires to the numerous streets off Patrick Street up to 10.30 a.m. on Sunday morning, having been on duty from 7 a.m. on the previous day.

Mr. Delaney, City Engineer, kindly came to my assistance and supervision of the men at work the various points required.

In connection with the fires at Dillon's Cross I wish to say that on receipt of the call for that fire I got in touch with the military at Victoria Barracks and asked them to take their hose reel and stand-pipes at the barrack gate down at once as I had been called to Grant's fire in Patrick Street, but they took no notice of my request. At the

Patrick Street fires it is remarkable that the military never brought any fire appliances whatever – as they had done on nearly all previous occasions up to the last few months. I must say that prior to these incendiary fires the military frequently rendered us valuable assistance not only in keeping the streets clear but also in extinguishing the fires. The statements of the two firemen working at Scully O'Connell's fire indicate the general position of the military on this occasion.

I have no hesitation in stating I believe all the above fires were incendiary fires and that a considerable amount of petrol or some such inflammable spirit was used in one and all of them. In some cases explosives were also used and persons were seen to go into and come out of the structures after breaking an entrance into same, and in some cases that I have attended the people have been brought out of their houses and detained in by-lanes until the fire had gained great headway. I have some of the petrol tins left behind in my possession.

I remain,

Your obedient servant,

ALFRED J. HUTSON.

APPENDIX 4

**Incident Report about the Burning of Cork issued by the RIC
District Inspector for Cork South**

District Inspector's Office
Cork South. 15–12–1920.

I beg to report that between 9.-30 p.m. and 5½ a.m. on the night
11–12th December the following houses and premises in Cork South
were maliciously set on fire:

1.	Alexander Grant & Co., Drapers	52 to 54	Patrick St., Cork.
2.	The Munster Arcade, Drapers,	28, 29, & 30	do.
3.	Cash & Co., Drapers,	18 to 21	do.
4.	The City Hall and Carnegie Library adjoining, situated in Albert Quay and Anglesea St.		

From the three former premises the fires appear to have spread to
adjoining premises and resulted in the destruction of the buildings
shown on the lists attached. I also attach a cutting form the *Cork
Examiner* of the 14th instant giving an expert survey of the area
of destruction by Mr. P. Delaney, the City Engineer. With the lists
already referred to this will help to show the extent of the damage.
The area destroyed comprises the principal business houses in Cork,
and the damage amounts, so far as can be estimated, to about three
million pounds. Fortunately no loss of life is known to have occurred
in the huge conflagration, and I think this fortunate aspect is entirely
due to the efforts of the Fire Brigade and Military and Police who

were on duty during the night, who went from house to house in the danger zone, and warned the inmates and helped them to leave before the fire extended to their houses.

I should say that prior to the starting of these fires there was considerable commotion in various parts of the City arising from rifle firing and the explosion of bombs. Early in the evening about 7.30 p.m. a party of Auxiliary Police had been ambushed at Dillon's Cross, near the Military Barracks. Bombs thrown at them wounded 12 of them, one of whom has since died. Other parties of Auxiliaries on duty in various parts of the City or returning to Barracks were fired upon, and returned the fire, and this intermittent firing continued up to 10 p.m. when the Curfew troops came on duty in the City.

The first of the fires broke out in the premises of Alexander Grant & Co. about 9.30 p.m. It was observed by a patrol of Police under a Head Constable as they were on duty at the head of George's St. adjoining the Grand Parade. The Head Const. i/c repaired to Tuckey St. Police Station, a short distance away, and, phoned to the Fire Brigade, and also to Union Quay Police Bks., the Headquarters of the City force, and with his force of 3 Sgts. and 11 Consts. he immediately went to the scene of the fire. He was there joined by a Head Const. and some Police from Cornmarket Street. Station and shortly afterwards by Captain Moran, D.I. and a party of 28 Sgts. and Constables from Union Quay. The Fire Brigade arrived without unnecessary delay, but the conflagration had already assumed such proportions that their efforts were mainly directed to checking the spread of the fire. The Police gave every possible assistance to the Brigade.

While the efforts of the Police and Brigade were concentrated on the fire in Grants an explosion was heard further down the street, and almost immediately after – about 12.15 a.m. – it was noticed that the premises of the Munster Arcade were on fire. It was impossible for the Fire Brigade to leave Messers Grant's premises at this time and although a party of Police from the main body were detached to go to this new fire, they were unable to do little further than warn the inmates of houses adjoining who appeared to be in danger. While they were thus engaged, their attention was attracted by explosions in the direction of Cash and Co. and these premises went quickly ablaze as in other cases.

The fires spread with alarming rapidity, and the resources of the Fire Brigade were entirely unable to cope with it. Parties detailed by the Officer i/c Curfew, with the aid of appliances available from the Fire Brigade stock, did everything possible to check the spread of the flames in the areas which could not be attended by the Fire Brigade, but it was obvious from the extent of the fire now raging, and the areas affected, that the destruction of huge blocks of buildings was inevitable and the efforts of all who helped in trying to check the fires were only partially successful.

Between 3 a.m. and 5 a.m. the City Hall was set on fire. This fire extended to the Carnagie Library. A party of Police from Union Quay were detailed to assist the members of the Fire Brigade who were on duty in the City Hall to check this fire. They assisted in removing some furniture and effects belonging to the Librarian from the premises, and in bringing some fire appliances from the Brigade operating in Patrick St. but even these were of little avail, the fire spread so rapidly and the extensive Hall and Library were practically completely destroyed.

It is not known how all these fires were caused but it is obvious that some highly flammable substance or liquid must have been extensively used considering the rapidity with which the flames spread in each case. The explosions which were heard rather indicated that petrol and bombs were used.

As to the motive for all these fires I think it must be assumed that they were in the nature of reprisals for the cowardly attack on the Auxiliary Police force earlier in the night. It is fairly apparent, however, that it was the work of a small number of individuals acting on a prearranged plan, and under the cover of the state of general excitement which prevailed during the night, who went from house to house setting them on fire. If a large number had participated they must have come under the notice of the Police or Military who were on duty.

If this had been the work of the Auxiliaries as a reprisal for the murderous attack which was made upon them earlier in the evening, it is reasonable to assume that it would have been carried out by a number of exasperated men who were prepared to take the consequences of doing it openly. If any large number of men were thus operating they would inevitably have come under the notice of Police or Military on duty, but they did not.

The conduct of the Police on the night in question, came prominently under the notice of some of the City Officials, and I think there will be no unfavourable comment on their action when the whole matter is inquired into. Every possible step was taken, the details of which I need not enter here, to see that they were properly under control, and that their actions and conduct in the practically unprecedented circumstances which had arisen would be in consonance with the long tradition of the Force, and would be untiringly devoted to the protection of the life and property of the Citizens.

The origin of the night's proceedings is therefore a mystery for the present. Later on evidence or information may be forthcoming which will elucidate it. Persons most clearly concerned are very reticent at present in communicating with the Police notwithstanding the charges and suggestions which are apparently very freely being communicated to other quarters.

In addition to the house burned on the occasion which I have shown on list 'A', attached a number of other houses shown on list 'B' were considerably damaged by fire, while those on list 'C' were wrecked and looted.

Considering the wide area concerned the Forces available were not adequate to prevent what occurred. One arrest for looting was made by the Police, and at about 5 a.m. on the morning of the 12th the Police had to disperse a large crowd of civilian looters who made a raid on goods already salved from one of the wrecked buildings.

Since the fires and wrecking the Police are practically continually on duty to prevent further looting of the wrecked buildings. That this was summarily checked in its early stages has however, eased the situation for the Police, and the stringent order issued by the G.O.C. in Cork regarding looting has further lessened their responsibilities.

I am glad to say that the efforts of the Police in this special direction has met with unqualified approval from the Citizens and the Order of the G.O.C. was timely and much appreciated.

2 D. I.

List 'A'

List of Premises destroyed in Cork by fire:

1.	J. O'Sullivan & Co., Tobacconist	12	Patrick St.
2.	J. Woulfe, Ladies' Outfitter,	13	do.
3.	Roches Stores, General Drapers	14 & 15	do.
4.	Lee Boot Manufacturing Co.	16	do.
5.	Scully O'Connell & Co., Children's Outfitters	17	do.
6.	Cash & Co. Ltd, Drapers & Gnl. Warehouse	18 to 21	do.
7.	T. Thompson & Co., Hosiery & Fancy W–house	22	do.
8.	R. Cudmore, Fruitier	22 A	do.
9.	Burton & Co., Men's Outfitters	23	do.
10.	Saxone & Sorosis, Shoe Co.	24	do.
11.	R. & J. Mckechnie, Dyers	25	do.
12.	O'Regan & Co., Hosiers &c.	26	do.
13.	Brooke Huges, Photographer	27	do.
14.	Munster Arcade, Drapers & Gnl Warehouse	28-30,	do.
15.	R. Sunner, Chemist	31	do.
16.	W. Egan & Sons	32	do.
17.	Forrest & Co., Silk Merchants	33 & 34	do.
18.	Haynes & Sons, Watchmakers &c.	51	do.
19.	A. Grant & Co., Drapers	52 to 54	do.
20.	James Hackett, Jeweller	55	do.
21.	Mrs Frewen, Vintner	25	Merchant's St.
22.	Miss O'Shea, Dress & Mantle Warerooms	22	Maylor St.
23.	Robert Walsh, Vintner	23	do.
24.	Cash & Co., Upholstery Warehouse	24 & 25	do.
25.	J. Ryan Ltd., Paper Merchants	26	do.

26.	D. Sullivan, Brush Maker	27	do.
27.	J. W. Creen & Co., Corn Merchants	28	do.
28.	Lee Cinema, Picture House	1& 2 Winthrop St.	
29.	Tomkins & Sons Ltd., Wine & Spirit Mchts	19	do.
30.	Tyler & Sons, Boot Shop	20 Winthrop St.	
31.	M. Murphy, Fruitier	21	do.
32.	Munster Arcade, Laundry	3 Robert St.	
33.	Shandon Printing Works	4 to 6	do.
34.	D. Mulcahy, Iron Works	8	do.
35.	Hagan Maurice, Barber	9	do.
36.	Patrick Noonan, Vintner	1–2 Cook Street	
37.	E. Woods, Wine & Spirit Merchants	3	do.
38.	Cashman & Co. do. & Grocers	4	do.
39.	P. O'Connor, Restaurant	5	do.
40.	Michael Martin, Fruitier	6	do.
41.	Miss O'Shea, Tobacconist	34 Georges St.	
42.	Miss Herlihy, News Agent	35	do.
43.	Munster Arcade, Cabinet Factory	36	do.
44.	M. Doyle, Vintner	37	do.
45.	K. Ahern	96	do.
46.	C. Bateman, Boot Factory	97	do.
47.	H. J. O'Callaghan, Vintner	98	do.
48.	Munster Arcade (runs through from Patk St.)	99	do.
49.	Patrick Forde, Vintner	103	do.
50.	E. McGrath, Farrier	Morgan St.	
51.	Messers Marah's, Garage		do.
52.	John Daly & Co., Wine & Spirit Merchants	Caroline St.	
53.	W. Mackessy, Vintner	6 Market Lane	
54.	J. O'Sullivan, Dining Rooms	4	do.
55.	T. Kinneally, Vintner	7	do.
56.	City Hall	Albert Quay	
57.	Carnegie Library	Anglesea St.	

LIST 'B'

Premises badly damaged by fire

1.	M. Nagle, Victuallar	38 George's St.
2.	J. Fitzgerald, Creamery	104 do.
3.	J. T. O'Sullivan, Chemist	105 do.
4.	N. Cahill, Tobacconist	106 do.
5.	L. L. Furguson, Hairdresser &c.	3 Winthrop St.
6.	J. Waters & Sons, Oil & Colour Warehouse	4 do.
7.	Power Bros., Merchant Tailors, Hatters &c.	5 do.
8.	T. Tierney, Fancy Fair	15 do.
9.	Scannell & Dowling, Provision Merchants	16 do.
10.	M. F. O'Shea, Tobacconist	16 A do.
11.	Cummins & Co., Ladies Outfitter	17 do.
12.	Hanley & Sons, Victuallers	17 A do.
13.	Joshua Manley, Provision Dealer	18 do.
14.	James Ryan, Stores	Merchant St
15.	Cork Furniture Stores	do.
16.	Messers Marsh, Auctioneer Offices	Morgan St.
17.	D. F. O'Sullivan & Co. Ltd., Tea Merchants	Maylor St.
18.	D. O'Sullivan, Stores	do.
19.	Thomas Molloy, Lodging House	do.
20.	W. Clifford	do.

List 'C'

Houses wrecked and looted

1. P. D. Buckley, Tobacconist	3 Grand Parade Buildgs	
2. Farmers Union Rooms	Marlboro St.	
3. Offices of 'Irish Times' Newspaper	do.	
4. Y.M.C.A. Hall	do.	
5. Munster Type Writing Co.	do.	
6. J. Kingston, Vintner	do.	
7. D. Wilson, Painter &c.	do.	
8. Cowhie Bros, Provision Merchants	82 George's St.	
9. D. Flynn, Draper	83	do.
10. F. V. Tadman, Hairdresser	55	do.
11. Mrs. Murphy, Tobacconist	58	do.
12. Gerald Griffin Boot Factory	59	do.

APPENDIX 5

Letter issued by Father Dominc to Florence O'Donoghue in the wake of the Decree of Excommunication issued by Bishop Daniel Cohalan on 12 December 1920

To: Brigade Adj.

A Cara dil: 12/12/20

I'm sure you have no difficulty with the Bishop's decree. Lest you might have, I'm sending you the following few points for your instruction and that of the Officers and men, generally.

An excommunication decree is one of the Church's censures or punishments for violation of a law (Canon 2255). This law may either be the Law of God, the Law of the Church, or a particular legitimate precept of an ecclesiastical legislation (Canon 2195 and 2198).

It may be inflicted only for an external and grievous (or mortal) violation of the law (Canon 2242).

Now, kidnapping, ambushing and killing, ordinarily would be grave sins or violations of Law and, if these acts were being performed by the Volunteers as private persons (whether physical or moral) would fall under the Excommunication.

But they are doing them by and with the authority of the State – The Republic of Ireland. And the State has the right and duty to defend the lives and property of its citizens, and to punish, even with death, those who are aiming at the destruction of the lives or property of its citizens or itself. It has moreover, a right and duty to protect by every means in its power the liberty of the State and its citizens against the Army of Occupation of a Foreign power or unjustly present in the country.

Hence, these acts performed by Irish Volunteers (the Army of the Republic) are, not only not sinful, but are good and meritorious. And, therefore the Excommunication does not affect us. There is no need to worry about it. Let the Boys keep going to Mass and Confession and Communion as usual. Just as there is no necessity for telling a Priest in Confession that you went to Mass on Sundays, so there's no necessity to tell him one is in the I.R.A., or that one took part in an ambush, kidnapping etc.

I'm sorry I am away and wish to goodness I could get back.

Will you convey this message to the Boys. And keep up the pressure on the enemy.

My love and Blessing to all the Brigade Staff. God keep you and protect you all.

D. O'C Brigade Chaplain

APPENDIX 6

Two captured letters written by a member of K Company, Auxiliary Division RIC, who participated in the burning of Cork. Extracts from these letters subsequently appeared as an Auxiliary 'statement' in *Who Burnt Cork City?* published by The Irish Labour Party and Trade Union Congress.

16.12.20

Aux.Division,
RIC
Dunmanway
Co. Cork

My Darling Mother,

I have just received your letter of the 10th enclosed with one from Dorothy of the 12th. We came on here from Cork and are billeted in a workhouse – filthily dirty half of us are down with bronchitis. I am at present in bed, my camp bed which I fortunately brought with me recovering from a severe chill contracted on Saturday night last during the burning and looting of Cork in all of which I took perforce a reluctant part. We did it all night never mind how much the well intentioned Hamar Greenwood would excuse us. In all my life and in all of the tales of fiction I have read, I have never experienced such orgies of murder, arson and looting as I have witnessed during the past 16 days with the R.I.C Auxiliaries. It baffles description and we are supposed to be officers and gentlemen. There are quite a number of decent fellows and likewise a number of ruffians.

On our arrival here from Cork one of our heroes held up a car with a priest and a civilian in it and shot them both through the head without cause of provocation. We were very kindly received by the people but the consequences of this cold-blooded murder is that no one will come within a mile of us and all shops are closed.

The brute who did it has been sodden with drink for some time and has been sent to Cork under arrest for examination by reporting lunacy. If certified sane he will be court-martialled and shot. The poor old priest was 65 and everybody's friend.

The burning and sacking of Cork followed immediately on the ambush of our men. I, as orderly Sergeant had to collect 20 men for a raid and they left barracks in two motor cars. I did not go as I was feeling sickly. The party had not gone 100 yards from barracks when bombs were thrown at them from over a wall. One dropped in a car and wounded 8 men one of whom has since died.

Very naturally the rest of the coy were enraged. The houses in the vicinity of the ambush were set alight and from there the various parties set out on their mission of destruction. Many who witnessed similar scenes in France or Flanders say that nothing they had experienced was comparable to the punishment meted out to Cork.

Reprisals are necessary and loyal Irishmen agree to that but there is a lot which should not be done, of course it is frequently unavoidable that the innocent suffer with the guilty. The sooner the Irish extremists recognise that they will not gain their point by the methods they deploy the better it will be for this unfortunate and misguided country.

You ask what our uniform is. The R.I.C Auxiliary uniform is khaki tunic and breeches and puttees, dark military greatcoat, dark green tam-o'-shanter and harp badge. Harp badges on collar of tunic. Revolver, rifle, bayonet and bombs complete our equipment.

I am up today (Friday) feeling a lot better but the accumulated chills have made this appearance on my face which is plastered from forehead to Adams apple with 'cold spots'. I am not beautiful to behold with a week's growth on my face and no immediate prospect of getting it off.

We had a lot of guard duty to do about four nights in each week, 24 hours on duty at a time, and no sleep at all for the sergeant of the guard who has got to post the sentries every 2 hours – that's me – I maintain we would not be overpaid at £5 *per diem*. It is the hardest life I have ever stuck but we get used to everything in time. A General Higginson arrived this morning to have a 'straight talk' to us about discipline etc., as he put it. I am afraid we struck terror into him for the 'straight talk' never materialised. He was most amiable. I could tell you much more but sufficient for the day etc.

The weather has been bitterly cold but the frost gave this morning. I wish this play was set in the Cameroons or somewhere near the equator, then I wouldn't mind it much. The country round here is quite poorly and very hilly. Our friends the gunmen are in their holes and we are here to round them up. They may or may not remain to face the ordeal.

It is well that you know everything. I have named Monica as my next-of-kin. Ireland has to pay very substantially for every RIC casualty. A mere flesh wound is paid and so on up to £5,000 to a man's widow. The widow of a young fellow who was shot in a raid in which I took part in Dublin received the latter amount.

Please send me the papers about Dorothy's concert and give me all the gossip about it. With much love my darling Mother,

Charlie

K Company
Aux. Div. RIC
Dunmanway
County Cork

My Dear Edith,

Many thanks for your kind and interesting letter. I am glad you are getting on well in your cinema studies. It won't surprise me to hear that you make a good thing of it yet.

We are having a h___ of a time here. You will have read all about Cork. Suffice to say I was there and very actively employed to boot until the dawn on Sunday. I just escaped the ambush in which 8 of our boys were wounded but arrived later as a reinforcement. We took a sweet revenge.

I have had three days in bed in the filthy work-house in which we are billeted here suffering from an accumulation of chills. Half the company has bronchitis and small wonder but we hope for better things 'Christmas Day in the workhouse'. We have purchased 12 turkeys to cheer us. I am practically all right again and shaved a week's growth of hair off my face this morning.

The weather has been bitterly cold and careering round the country in open cars neither conduces to one's health nor comfort. You must forgive me for not writing to you again sooner & excuse delays in days to come for I don't know quite yet whether I am on my head or my heels. I will do my best but don't wait to hear from me when you have a little news to impart. Dorothy will be in Scotland for her 2nd concert which I hope will be as successful as the last.

With love and a kiss for yourself & Joyce,

Charlie

Please excuse writing
My hand is very shaky

Appendix 7

**Statements from D.I. Deignan of the RIC and Lt Col Latimer and
Lt De Havilland of K Company Auxiliary Division, RIC provided to
the RIC Inquiry into the Burning of Cork**

D. I. DEIGNAN states with reference to the Court of Enquiry on
the burning of Cork:

1. That he was handicapped by not having been present on the first
two days of the Enquiry, for which he was the R.I.C. member.

2. The Court consisted of Lt. Col. Stapleton, Major Parkers and
Major Kerns. There was a major Milton present who seemed to be a
lawyer; he was not a member of the Court but he was there practically all
the time interrogating witnesses. This, in his opinion, was most irregular.
The procedure of taking evidence was as follows:–Witness would come in
and Colonel Stapleton would ask him what he had to say about it. After
he had made his statement the evidence was typed in Colonel Stapleton's
words and not in the words of the witness. D. I. Deignan states that he
sometimes asked questions and got answers from witnesses and neither
question nor answer was put down. He states that Colonel Stapleton
showed no bias at all, and his attitude throughout was perfectly fair.

3. His reasons for objecting to the finding were: – 'K' Company's
first platoon arrived in Cork 2nd December, the last platoon arrived 8th
December; they were living in barracks and some sleeping on the floor of
the gymnasium; there was absolutely no accommodation for Headquarters,
therefore it was very unjust to blame the O.C. of 'K' Company, Colonel
Latimer, for living at the Imperial Hotel. High authority was blamed
without evidence. This is contrary to British Law.
He further stated:

I asked one witness who talked about 'Black and Tans' and R.I.C. and Auxiliaries, how he distinguished between these, he said by uniforms only. There is a large number of uniforms in the possession of ex-soldiers and Sinn Féiners. My point is, that unless the individuals are recognised, uniforms are not sufficient proof.

I understand there were 2,433 soldiers in Cork on the night of 11th December, this appears ample force to have prevented Cork being burnt. It does not appear to have been used. My opinion is that 'K' Company could not possibly have been in a position to pick out particular houses to burn as they had only been a few days in Cork. Colonel Latimer seems to have done his best to control and account for his men. I think it is possible that some odd members of K Company were implicated in the burnings; there is no proof as to individuals, and therefore, legally, it is impossible to bring the charges home. There is no evidence to show that more than one soldier was implicated, and he was a soldier in kilts. In my opinion, people are not likely to give evidence against soldiers before a military tribunal.

Before the finding there was no consultation between the members before the evidence was complete. The President wrote down the finding himself, and the other members of the Court agreed to it. I did not agree to it and declined to sign it. I asked one member if he thought it was fair to censure authority behind his back, i.e. without hearing his case, he agreed it was not fair, but still signed the finding. I think there should have been two police officers on the Court. I told the Court that Sir Hamar Greenwood was a lawyer, and he would not, having read the evidence, have agreed with the finding.

Lieut Colonel LATIMER states:–

1.   The case was already prejudged by the action of the military authorities in clearing the Police off the streets at 3 a.m.; it was then that the looting began. It was also prejudiced by sending 'K' Company out of Cork the next day.

2. A Military Court judging a matter of that kind is bound to be unconsciously prejudiced. Civilian witnesses I asked to be called were not, as far as I know, called. Kitchen was one and Freeman of the Imperial Hotel another. Kitchen's evidence was particularly important as his house had been burnt down by Shinners two or three days previously. Both these men can testify to the work done by me and the Company under my commanding fighting the fire.

3. I collected 55 men in Victoria Barracks, where I went as soon as I heard of the ambush. I took them in a formed body on foot at 10 o'clock with the curfew party, and then to the Bridewell. There can not have been more than six men of the Auxiliary division in the town, apart from this party. There were Constable Veterans of my Company on duty at Victoria Barracks. The remaining 6 should not have been able to get out as a military guard had orders not to let any of my company out without a pass, or unless in a formed body under an officer. The soldiers are mostly confined to barracks by day and take no active part in patrolling Cork. They live the life of a besieged garrison and are only allowed in a protected area. I saw several soldiers drinking in the early morning of the 12th (during the night of the fire) between 2 and 3 a.m. I applied for accommodation for myself and office in Victoria Barracks. I could get none. I had to live outside and chose the Imperial Hotel so as to be near Union Quay Barracks, where I used the Divisional Commissioner's Office.

Mr. HAVILAND, Platoon Commander, 'K' Company, states:-

I was in the ambush at Dillon's Cross, and I saw glares of burning houses within 5 minutes of the ambush. It was quite impossible for any of the Auxiliary Division to have done this as a result of the ambush. My own impression is that it was pre-arranged by the Shinners, to start fire after the ambush.

Lt. Colonel LATIMER further states:-

No car of 'K' Co's transport left Victoria Barracks until the next day, after the fire. I got the gas turned off at 3 a.m. as this seemed a reason for the fire spreading. I did this by telephoning the gas authorities, but they objected as I was not the C.M.A. I had to use threats to get the gas turned off. If 'K' Company, Auxiliary Division, is accused, I demand a judicial inquiry by impartial Judges of the English Bench. I consider no proper action was taken by the Military Authorities to get the fires under control, and it was left to a handful of Auxiliary Police and R.I.C. to do what they could to check the fires and stop looting. The whole 55 men of my party were working in sections under my supervision 'til 3 a.m. when I sent the majority of them back to barracks as the Police were ordered off the streets by the Military authorities. My men did not know their way about the streets and they could not have sufficient knowledge to have burnt the houses if chosen. The Cork Savings Bank and another bank near the Mall were guarded by my patrols. Fires had been occurring in Cork 10 days previous to the arrival of "K" Company.

Capt. Hutson of the Cork Fire Brigade, stated that on the occasion of one of these burnings a hose pipe had been cut and his men fired on by Auxiliaries. This appears in the Minutes of the Water Board. This clearly shows ignorance and prejudice. The Auxiliary Company is the first body to reinforce the Army's Regulations. They thus incurred the very strong hatred of the Cork Shinners. I found some of the R.I.C. joined on to my party, they said they were going with me and they were Auxiliaries, I said they were not, and told them to get away out of it to Union Quay Barracks.

9.1.21.

APPENDIX 8

Pastoral Letter from Bishop Daniel Cohalan read in all churches in the Roman Catholic Diocese of Cork on Sunday, 19 December 1920

Very Reverend and Reverend Fathers, and Beloved Brethren

In the presence of the ruin of a great part of our City of Cork the pastoral duty impels me to address to you a statement about the crimes that have been committed in the dioceses, crimes by the people and crimes against the people and crimes by agents of the Government; to condemn and deplore these crimes and, in order to prevent a repetition of these crimes in future, to protect the lives and property of innocent people, to notify again a decree of excommunication which I have already promulgated against those who should be guilty of those crimes within the diocese in future.

We were singularly free in this diocese from the crimes of murder until about the middle of March. But policemen had been shot here and there throughout the country, and the police believed that the murder of their men was a studied and settled part of Volunteer policy. A general meeting of policemen was called by someone in the city; a resolution was proposed that if any policemen were shot in the city, one of the leading Volunteers should be shot by way of reprisals; and I am glad to say that the resolution was defeated. Later on a clique succeeded in carrying out the wicked project which the general body of police had refused to accept. On March 19–20 the terrible reprisal murder of Lord Mayor MacCurtain took place; and since then it has become a devils competition in feats of murder and arson between members of the Volunteer organisation and agents of the Crown. It will be constructive to consider some of the features of these crimes.

Constable Murtagh was murdered on Pope's Quay on the night of the Lord Mayor's murder, but earlier in the night; and it is certain it was the murder of Constable Murtagh that gave occasion to the Murder of the Lord Mayor. Who murdered Constable Murtagh? One theory was that he was murdered by the police for refusing to take part in the Lord Mayor's murder; but the theory was absolutely false. Then it was said that the dead constable's face was found to be blackened as if he had prepared himself for a crime; but the statement was a cruel calumny on a dead man. Again, it was stated that material for blackening his face had been found in the dead constable's pocket; but this, like the preceding statement was a gross calumny of a murdered man. Who, then, murdered Constable Murtagh? It was not known at the time of the murder; but now the irresponsibles by whom he was murdered are more than suspected; and it is these irresponsibles who brought on the murder of the Lord Mayor by agents of the Government of the same night. As in the case of Constable Murtagh, so at every later murder of policemen a false theory was at once started; that the policeman deserved his fate, that he had himself committed murder, that it was he who had murdered a boy in bed; and by these false theories the conscience of the people was drugged and their horror of the murders considerably lessened. Some probably, too, will say nothing occurred at Dillon's Cross; but fables are poor consolation to the sufferers of the burning of Patrick street.

And leaving out of count for a moment the moral issue. I would ask you what has the country gained politically by the murder of policemen and by the burning of barracks and of historical or costly buildings. Some Republicans used to speak of the receding authority of England and of the occupation of deserted districts by the advancing authority of the Republic when some policemen were murdered and their barracks burned. He would be a bold Republican who would talk now in a city or county of districts delivered from British rule. No.

– the killing of policemen was morally murder and politically of no consequence, and the burning of barracks was simply the destruction of Irish property.

Recently ambushes have taken place at Kilmichael and Dillon's Cross with serious loss of life, and with terrible after consequences to the unoffending community. The ambushers came from nobody knows where, and when they have done their work disappear – nobody knows to what destination. Ordinarily, there is very little risk to the ambushers themselves as there is no risk in shooting a policeman from behind a screen. But by this time boys and men taking part in ambushes must know that by their criminal act they are exposing perhaps a whole countryside, perhaps a town or city, to the danger of terrible reprisals. When the ambushers disappear into safety they leave the lives and the homes and the property of innocent people unprotected and undefended, to the mercy of reprisals at the hands of servants of the government. That is not very valiant. In battle, these men would be the bravest of the brave. But again, it is not valiant to execute an ambush and then go off and leave a countryside or city to the terrible danger of reprisals.

Terrible reprisals appear to have been determined on after the massacre in Kilmichael, following some kidnappings and other offences. When or where the reprisals would fall remained altogether unknown. The immediate pretext or occasion was a matter of indifference. But as the murder of Constable Murtagh created the occasion for the murder by servants of the Crown of Lord Mayor MacCurtain, so the ambush at Dillon's Cross supplied the pretext and immediate occasion for the destruction of Patrick Street. But, as I have said, the pretext and occasion were immaterial; the destruction of Patrick Street had already been determined on. But, taking occasion from the ambush at Dillon's Cross the servants of the Government attacked the city on Saturday night, and the city suffered more damage at their hands than Dublin suffered during the Rebellion of 1916.

We are face to face with the crimes of individuals and with Government crimes. The crimes of the Government in Ireland are on a different plane, and are infinitely greater than the crimes of a private military organisation because it is the duty of the Government, through its servants to protect the lives and property of the citizens, especially innocent, unoffending citizens. But instead of defending the lives and property of the innocent, the Government, by a carefully laid plan, for which not even a cloak of legality has been provided, has conducted through its servants a reprisal campaign of murder of the innocent and of the destruction of their property. With the view of procuring the submission of the Republican army by terrorism exercised over the innocent and unoffending. The plan was carefully laid and carried out with all the forces of the Government. Curfew was put on, and in this way witnesses of nocturnal Government crime were removed from the streets; and then the servants of the Government were loose to murder and to burn. And in this connection it must be noted that almost every answer given by ministers in the House of Commons to questions about these outrages in Ireland has been a falsehood. An invading power which claimed no authority over the country, could not commit greater crimes in Ireland than those which are committed by British Forces with the more than tacit approval of the British Government. Before the recent burning, and the murder of the Delanys, we had the murder of Mr. Coleman, of Eugene O'Connell and the boy Hanlon committed by servants of the Crown. The Curfew makes proof difficult. But there is convincing proof in the case of Mr. Coleman; and if I have not referred hitherto publicly to these murders it is because with the approval of Mr. Coleman's widow and friends, I waited first until the military investigation should have taken place, and, secondly, until the affidavits, which were being prepared, were put at my disposal.

The killing of an individual is murder, and ambushes are murderous. Some complain if in the same discourse I condemn the murder of a policeman and of a civilian; others complain if, when condemning murder, I condemn bad government, coercion and reprisals. But murder is murder, and arson is arson, whether committed by agents of the Government or by members of the Republican army, and it is the duty of a Bishop to denounce murder and arson, from whatever source they come. Then there is danger of becoming familiar with murder and arson; there is what is called blood-lust and fire-lust; men can come to look upon an enemy, especially in time of war, as a sportsman would look upon game or on a wild animal. An Irish Parliament will have charge of her own police. The Volunteer police are now universally and deservedly popular and esteemed. But there will be criminals in Irish society who won't love the police; and it would be disastrous in the Ireland of the future if the habit of shooting obnoxious policemen were allowed to continue.

In the awful circumstances in which we live, to protect our men and boys from the danger of murder and arson, and to protect the community at large from the evil of reprisals, I notify again to the faithful of the dioceses, through the different churches, the following decree of excommunication, which has already been promulgated and is already in force:-

Besides the sinfulness of the acts from their opposition to the law of God, anyone, be he a subject of this dioceses or an extern, who, within this dioceses of Cork, shall organise or take part in ambushes or kidnapping, or shall otherwise be guilty of murder or attempted murder, shall incur by the very fact the censure of excommunication.

+DANIEL COHALAN

Bishop of Cork.

(Witness) PATRICK CANON SEXTON

Farranferris, 12th Dec., 1920

Some of the Corporators have thought fit to criticise this decree of excommunication, and to express surprise that I did not issue instead, a condemnation of the burning and a message of sympathy with the citizens of Cork. Some would like at the present moment to divert public attention from the spectacle of what, until a few days ago, was Patrick Street; from the awful destruction which, though beyond doubt the criminal work of agents of the Government, was occasioned by recent kidnappings and tragic ambushes; and divert attention, too, from the consequences of the false teachings of persons who should know better, that Ireland is at the moment a sovereign independent State, and that consequently Irishmen have authority to kill England's forces and to burn English property in Ireland. Patrick Street is an ugly, and to these teachers, disquieting, consequence of their false and immoral teaching.

The excommunication decree adds nothing to the Divine Law. It includes an ecclesiastical prohibition by Divine Law, and adds the sanction of severe ecclesiastical penalties. What is prohibited and punished by the excommunication? First, murder, no matter by whom committed, is prohibited and punished; and why should the Corporators and their lay theologians rage because murder is punished? Next, attempt at murder is punished; and again, why should the Corporators and their lay theologians murmur if punishment is decreed for attempt at murder? In the third place, murderous ambushes are punished; and how could the Corporators and their lay theologians defend murderous ambushes? And finally, kidnapping, whether it leads to murder or to simple detention is punished; and again, why should the Corporators and their lay theologians be angry if kidnapping is forbidden and punished? The excommunication goes no further.

I appeal at this time of Christmas to all Volunteers, privates and officers, to as many as believe in the Divinity of Jesus Christ, to bow to the teachings of the Gospel, to remember the Divine Commandment, 'Thou Shalt Not Kill', to respect human life, to have consideration for the unprotected general public, neither to give nor to obey any order that would subject them to the terrible effects of excommunication.

I ask you all, priests and people, to pray for an honourable political settlement which may enable all the children of Ireland to work harmoniously and contentedly for the betterment of our country; and which, if it be not complete, will lay down the lines on which the country can advance by peaceful evolution to its full ideal of freedom.

+DANIEL COHALAN
Bishop of Cork
Fourth Sunday of Advent, 1920

APPENDIX 9

Weekly summaries of outrages against the police, 28/11/20 –12/12/20

SUMMARY OF OUTRAGES AGAINST THE POLICE reported during the week ended 5th December,1920: also the number of similar outrages reported during the week ended 28th November, 1920.

Nature of Outrage	Reference Page	No. for week 5.12.20	No. for week 28.11.20	Increase or Decrease	
Policemen killed	1	19	2	+ 17	16 details
" wounded	1. 2.	5	7	- 2	1 .
" threatened	–	–	4	- 4	
" attacked but not injured............	3. 4	5	7	- 2	
Police pensioners threatened	5	1	1	—	
" candidates "	–	–	–	–	
Policemen's families threatened or attacked.............	6.	1	1	—	
Policemen's tradesmen,landlords, threatened or attacked.	7	3	1	+ 2	
Police property damaged........	–	–	3	- 3	
TOTAL		34	26	+ 8	
Number of arrests in connection with above outrages.....................		–	1	- 1	

INCREASE or DECREASE in R.I.C. strength during week.....

Total strength on 28th November,1920..................... 11,853

Deaths during week (reported)... 5

Retirements during week......... 53

Resignations (Applications)..... 30

Dismissals or Discharged......... 3

Total wastage during week....... 91

Recruits joined:-
From Ireland............ 22   Including 6 B'men

Great Britain........ 214   28 B'

Total 236

Net Increase or Decrease during week.................. 145

Total strength on 5th December,1920..................... 11,998

Number of temporary cadets not included in above - 82.

SUMMARY OF OUTRAGES AGAINST THE POLICE reported during the
week ended 12th December, 1920; also the number of similar
outrages reported during the week ended 5th December, 1920.

Nature of outrage	Reference Page	No. for week 12.12.20	No. for week 5.12.20	Increase or Decrease	
Policemen killed	–	–	19	– 19	
" wounded	1	13	5	+ 8	
" threatened	–	–	–		
" attacked but not injured.........	2	4	5	– 1	
Police pensioners threatened	–	–	1	– 1	
" candidates "	3	3	–	+ 3	
Policemen's families threatened or attacked..........	–	–	1	– 1	
Policemen's tradesmen, landlords, threatened or attacked.	4	1	3	– 2	
Police property damaged.......	5	5	–	+ 5	
TOTAL		26	34	– 8	
Number of arrests in connection with above outrages................		–	–	–	

INCREASE or DECREASE in R.I.C. strength during week

Total strength on 5th December, 1920.................. _11,998_

Deaths during week (reported).._____1_

Retirements during week....... _____8_

Resignations (Applications).... _44_

Dismissals or Discharged......... _____2_

Total wastage during week...... _55_

Recruits joined
From Ireland. _18_

Gt. Britain... _297_ Including 70 B'men.

Total _315_

Net Increase or Decrease during week................. _260_

Total strength on 12th December, 1920.................. _12,258_

Number of temporary cadets not included in above - 156.

SUMMARY OF OUTRAGES AGAINST THE POLICE reported during the
week ended 19th December, 1920: also the number of similar
outrages reported during the week ended 12th December, 1920.

Nature of Outrage	Reference Page	No. for week 19.12.20	No. for week 12.12.20	Increase or Decrease
Policemen killed	1	7	—	+ 7
" wounded	1. 2.	7	13	- 6
" threatened	—	—	—	—
" attacked but not injured.........	3	5	4	+ 1
Police pensioners threatened	—	—	—	—
" candidates "	—	—	3	- 3
Policemen's families threatened or attacked.............	4	2	—	+ 2
Policemen's tradesmen, landlords, threatened or attacked.	5	3	1	+ 2
Police property damaged........	6	4	5	- 1
TOTAL		28	26	+ 2
Number of arrests in connection with above outrages.....................		8	—	+ 8

INCREASE or DECREASE IN R.I.C. strength during week

Total strength on 12th December, 1920................... 12,258

Deaths during week (reported).. __2__

Retirements during week........ __11__

Resignations (Applications).... __21__

Dismissals or Discharged....... __5__

Total wastage during week..... __39__

Recruits Joined
From Ireland __27__

Gt. Britain.... __254__ Including 26 "B" men

Total __281__

Net Increase or Decrease during week..................... 242

Total strength on 19th December, 1920................. 12,500

Notes

1. Born at Ballyknockane, County Cork, on 20 March 1884, Tomás Mac-Curtain was a founding member of the Cork City Corps of Irish Volunteers in December 1913 becoming secretary of the provisional committee that governed the unit. During the Redmond split, he remained with the Irish Volunteers and in 1915 was appointed commandant of the re-organised Cork Brigade. Owing to a series of conflicting orders sent to Cork from Dublin in the week before the Easter Rising, MacCurtain mobilised his men as originally planned on Easter Sunday but stood them down that evening. The following week he negotiated an agreement with the British in Victoria Barracks whereby the arms and ammunition held by his men would be surrendered to the lord mayor of Cork for safe keeping. He and his men would in turn be guaranteed their freedom, but the British broke this agreement and MacCurtain and other leading Volunteers in his brigade were arrested and interned in Britain. He was released at Christmas 1916 but re-arrested two months later and again interned in Britain where he remained until 20 June 1917.

2   Born at North Main Street, Cork city, on 28 March 1879, Terence Mac-Swiney developed a love of Irish language and culture at an early age and was a founder member of the Cork Literary Society in January 1901. In 1908, he became a member of the Cork Dramatic Society and went on to write a series of poems and plays. He was also a founding member of the Cork City Corps of Irish Volunteers in December 1913 and was elected to the provisional committee. In September 1914, he founded his own newspaper, *Fianna Fáil*, which put forward the views of the leadership of the Irish Volunteers in the immediate wake of the Redmond split. In the summer of 1915, MacSwiney was appointed full time organiser for County Cork and P. S. O'Hegarty later wrote of him that 'in that capacity he was tireless and wonderful. All over County Cork he went on his bicycle and the living flame sprang up behind him'. In the aftermath of the Easter Rising, MacSwiney was arrested and deported to Britain where he remained until Christmas 1916. He was arrested again on 21 February 1917 and sent to England where he was held in open interment until the following June in a village named Bromyard on the border of Worcestershire.

    Seán O'Hegarty was born in Cork on 21 March 1881, and developed a passion for Irish culture at an early age. He was a committed republican and, following the resurgence of the IRB in Cork in 1906, he became the leader or 'Centre' of the Cork branch or 'Circle'. He was also the secretary of the 'O'Growney Branch' of the Gaelic League and by 1910 had become the chairman of the Cork branch of the National Council of Sinn Féin. Dissatisfied with a number of policies adopted by the party, O'Hegarty and his supporters left Sinn Féin the following year and the city branch was soon dissolved thereafter. O'Hegarty was also a founding member of the Cork Brigade of Volunteers but in October 1914 he was expelled from the city and *de facto* confined to Ballingeary under the terms of the Defence of the Realm Act. A confidant of both MacCurtain and MacSwiney throughout 1916, when the Cork Brigade was reorganised in 1917 O'Hegarty returned to prominence and became second-in-command to MacCurtain. However, unlike MacCurtain and MacSwiney, O'Hegarty had no desire to enter politics, believing instead that the military option was the only one which would ultimately succeed.

Florence O'Donoghue was born at Rathmore, County Kerry, on 21 July 1894, moved to Cork in 1910 and joined the Cork Brigade of Irish Volunteers in December 1916 after he heard of the death of his cousin, Patrick O'Connor, in the Easter Rising. Tomás MacCurtain clearly recognised O'Donoghue's organisational skills at an early stage and in 1917 he was appointed second-in-command of the unit's cyclist company. He was subsequently appointed brigade communications officer and, in 1918, he succeeded Pat Higgins as brigade adjutant.

3   Foy, Michael T., *Michael Collins – The Intelligence War* (Sutton Publishing, UK, 2006), p. 13.

4   Cork No. 1 Brigade covered the area of mid Cork. The brigade comprised ten battalions, two of which were located in Cork city with others centred at: Ballincollig, Cobh/Midleton, Whitechurch, Blarney/Donoughmore, Macroom, Ballyvourney, Rochestown/Crosshaven and Youghal.

Cork No. 2 Brigade covered the area of north Cork. Its boundaries extended from Ballynoe in the east to the Kerry border west of Millstreet and from the Mushera mountains in the south to the Limerick county boundary in the north. The brigade comprised seven battalions which were located at Fermoy, Mallow, Castletownroche, Charleville, Newmarket, Kanturk and Millstreet.

Cork No. 3 Brigade covered the area of west Cork. Its boundaries extended from Ballinhassig to the west and south-west of the county. The brigade comprised six battalions which were located in Bandon, Clonakilty, Dunmanway, Skibbereen, Bantry and Castletownbere.

5   Born in Cork in 1883, Dominic O'Connor was educated in the Christian Brothers school and Rochestown Monastery where he entered the Capuchin order in 1889. He was ordained on St Patrick's Day 1906 and

served as a chaplain in the British army during the First World War. He returned to Cork in 1917 and in 1918 was appointed chaplain to the Cork Brigade of Irish Volunteers. His brother Joseph was also a member of the Volunteers and held the appointment of brigade quartermaster in Cork No. 1 Brigade.

6   Sinn Féin won 73 seats in the 1918 general election. Thirty-four deputies had been imprisoned before the meeting of the first Dáil and the others were unable to attend.

7   Abbott, Richard, *Police Casualties in Ireland 1919–1922* (Mercier Press, Cork 2000), p. 67.

8   Foy, *Michael Collins*, p. 22.

9   Born on 3 August 1869, Strickland was commissioned into the Norfolk Regiment in 1888. He served in Upper Burma (1888–89), with the Egyptian Army (1889–1905), in India (1906) and Nigeria (1906–14). He served in France for the duration of the First World War. In 1914 he was appointed officer commanding, the 1st Battalion, the Manchester Regiment. In 1916 he was given command of the 1st Division which he held until he arrived in Victoria Barracks in 1919 to take over the 6th Division.

10   A native of Bannu, India where he was born on 10 November 1873 Higginson was educated at Saint Lawrence College, Ramsgate he later went on to attend Sandhurst and was commissioned into the Royal Dublin Fusiliers in 1894. He served in West Africa (1897–98), South Africa (1899–1902), in the Aden (1902) and the Blue Nile (1908). On the outbreak of the First World War Major Higginson was appointed Brigade Major of the 143rd Brigade and sent to the western front. In 1915 he took over the command of the 2nd Royal Dublin Fusiliers and in 1916 he was appointed commander of the 53rd Infantry Brigade. In the closing year of the war he took over command of the 12th Division. He held this appointment until 1919 when he arrived in Victoria Barracks to take command of the 17th Infantry Brigade.

11   Fred Murray informed his comrades that on the night of the shooting he had been in the company of Fr Gabriel Harrington, a well known and respected Capuchin priest. Fr Gabriel readily agreed to give evidence at the trial. He had been with Murray that night and knew that Fred had a knee injury at the time, which made it impossible for him to have been at the place where the shooting occurred. However the jury at the Cork summer assizes failed to agree on a verdict. J. Travers Wolfe, the crown solicitor, then made an application to have the case transferred to Dublin on the basis that the Cork jury had been canvassed and intimidated before the trial. When Murray's case was heard in Dublin's Green Street courthouse

he was found guilty and sentenced to twelve months' imprisonment. The view adopted by Fr Gabriel's religious superiors at that time is illustrated by the fact that within a week of Murray's trial he was transferred to the United States.

12   The O'Donoghue Papers, MS. 31, 124 (2).

13   Foy, *Michael Collins*, p. 28.

14   *Ibid.*

15   Leahy, Michael, Witness Statement (WS) No 1421 Bureau of Military History (BMH).

16   The O'Donoghue Papers MS 31,124 (2).

17   Michael Kenny's War of Independence Pension Application.

18   A detailed account of the Quinlisk case can be found in Florence O'Donoghue's biography of Tomás MacCurtain, p. 164 and *Florence and Josephine O'Donoghue's War of Independence* by John Borgonovo (ed.), (Irish Academic Press, Dublin 2006) pp. 67–75.

19   Murray, Patrick, Witness Statement (WS) No. 1584, Bureau of Military History (BMH).

20   The O'Donoghue Papers, 31,124 (2).

21   *Tomás MacCurtain, Soldier & Patriot*, Florence O'Donoghue, (Anvil Books, 1955) p. 171.

22   O'Donoghue Papers, MS 31, 430.

23   Feeley, Michael, WS no. 68, BMH.

24   Both Dan Breen and Florrie O'Donoghue confirm in later publications that MacCurtain was indeed present in Dublin during an aborted ambush attempt on Lord French in October 1920. This gives credibility to Feeley's account of the meeting on 19 March at Union Quay.

25   *Cork Examiner*, 23 March 1920.

26   Bennet, Richard, *The Black and Tans*, (Barnes and Noble), USA, 1995, p. 65.

27   *Cork Examiner*, 1 April 1920.

28   *Ibid.*

29   Born in 1862, Cecil Fredrick Nevil Macready had extensive experience in dealing with civil unrest. He had commanded both the police and military forces involved in the bitter coal strike that had gripped South Wales in 1910 and had been appointed commissioner of the London Metropolitan Police in 1918. He played a major part in settling the London police strike of 1919.

30   *Chronology of Events*, Vol III. BMH.

31   Harvey, Dan & White, Gerry, *The Barracks – A History of Victoria/Collins Barracks, Cork* (Mercier Press, Cork, 1997), p. 67.

32   Macready, General Sir Nevil, *Annals of an Active Life*, Vol II (Hutchinson

& Co. London 1927), p.482.

33   *Cork Examiner*, 17 August 1920.

34   *Ibid.*

35   Dónal O'Callaghan was a committed republican and fluent Irish speaker. Born in Cathedral Place, Cork, in 1892, he was also a member of the Irish Volunteers and held the position of second lieutenant in B Company, Cork City Battalion, at Easter 1916. He was well known for his talents as an orator and public speaker.

36   Once O'Hegarty took command of the brigade, Michael Leahy, the OC of the 4th Battalion was appointed vice-commandant

37   Murray, Patrick, WS No. 1584, BMH

38   *Ibid.*

39   Chavasse, Moirin, *Terence MacSwiney* (Clonmore and Reynolds, Dublin, 1961), p175.

40   *Cork Examiner,* 26 October 1920.

41   O'Donoghue, Florence, *No Other Law* (Anvil Books, Dublin, 1986), p. 99.

42   Calwell, C. E., *Field Marshall Sir Henry Wilson – His Life and Diaries,* Vol. II (Cassell & Co, London, 1927), pp. 263–264.

43   *Cork Examiner,* 3 October 1920; Abbott, *Police Casualties in Ireland,* p. 129.

44   *Cork Constitution,* 9 October 1920.

45   Poland, Pat, *'Firecall'! – Cork Fire Brigade Centenary Review 1877–1977* (The Society of St Florian, Cork, 1977), p. 32; the shift for the fireman on duty at the escape station on St Patrick's Street was 8 p.m. to 6 a.m. from May to August and 8 p.m. to 7 a.m. September to April.

46   *Cork Examiner,* 21 October 1920.

47   *Ibid.*

48   The Parliamentary Labour Party appointed three members to serve on the commission: Arthur Henderson, J. Lawson and W. Lunn. The Executive Committee of the Labour Party appointed its chairman, A. G. Cameron, its vice-chairman F. W. Jowett and J. Bromley. William Adamson joined Brigadier-General C. B. Thompson became military advisor and Captain C. W. Kendall, legal advisor. Tomas Johnson, secretary of the Irish Labour Party and Trade Union Congress was attached to the commission and the services of E. Rooney as stenographer was placed at the disposal of the Commission by the Irish Transport Worker's Union.

49   The composition of the American Commission on Ireland was: L. Hollingsworth Wood, chairman; Frederic C. Howe, vice-chairman; Jane Adams; James H. Maurer Major Oliver P. Newman; US Senator George W. Norris; Rev. Norman Thomas; US Senator David I. Walsh with William MacDonald and Harold Kellock as secretaries.

50   Charles Brown, *The Story of the 7th* (privately published, n.d.), p. 34.

51   General E. P. Strickland Papers: *History of the 6th Division in Ireland*, p. 61, Imperial War Museum London.

52   Crozier, Brig. Gen F .P., *Ireland For Ever* (Jonathan Cape, London, 1932), p. 175.

53   Abbott, Richard, *Police Casualties in Ireland*, pp. 311, 313; *Cork Constitution*, 22 November 1920.

54   *Cork Examiner*, 13 November 1920.

55   Bennett, Richard, *The Black and Tans* (Barnes and Nobel, New York, 1995) p. 115.

56   Quoted in Abbot, *Police Casualties in Ireland*

57   A romance later blossomed between Josephine Brown and Florrie O'Donoghue and the couple married in April 1921. A comprehensive account of the extraordinary circumstances that led to the relationship between Florrie O'Donoghue and Josephine Brown can be found in: *Florence and Josephine O'Donoghue's War of Independence*

58   Josephine O'Donoghue's War of Independence Pension Application (author's copy).

59   *Cork Examiner*, 1 February 1921.

60   List of IRA Executions 1920, Military Archives (MA); *Cork Examiner*, 17–18 November 1920 also Mick Murphy in the O'Malley Notebooks, UCD.

61   Mick Murphy in the O'Malley Notebooks.

62   *Cork Examiner*, 19 November, 1920.

63   *Ibid.*

64   *Ibid.* – A detailed account and analysis of what happened in Cork city on the night of 17/18 November 1920 is provided by Peter Hart in his book *The IRA and Its Enemies*.

65   Healy, Daniel, WS No. 1656, BMH.

66   *Cork Examiner*, 23 November 1920.

67   *Ibid.*, 22 November 1920.

68   *Ibid.*, 26 November 1920; 'IRA List of Executions 1920,' MA; Bride Downing to Dáil Minister for Defence, Cathal Brugha, 13 December 1921, MA, A/0535 VI.

69   *Cork Examiner*, 29 November 1920.

70   *Ibid.*, Saturday, 27 November and Monday 29 November 1920.

71   American Commission – Interim Report, p. 83.

72   *Cork Examiner*, 27 November 1920.

73   De Róiste Diaries, 27 November 1920, Cork Archives Institute (CAI).

74   A year later, Florence O'Donoghue reported to Gearóid O'Sullivan, the Volunteer adjutant-general: 'This man [Downing] was convicted and shot

as a spy in Cork on 28 November 1920'. MA, A/0535.

75   *Cork Examiner*, 30 November 1920.

76   While Tom Barry has always maintained that the surrender attempt by the Auxiliaries had been bogus, the matter of what transpired at Kilmichael on 28 November 1920 has been the subject of some intense debate among historians. For accounts of the Kilmichael ambush and the subsequent debate see: *Guerrilla Days in Ireland* and *The Reality of the Anglo-Irish War 1920–21* by Tom Barry; *Towards Ireland Free* by Liam Deasy; *Tom Barry – IRA Freedom Fighter* by Meda Ryan; *The IRA and Its Enemies – Violence and Community in Cork 1916–1923* by Peter Hart; *Kilmichael: The False Surrender* by the Aubane Historical Society and *The Origins and Organisation of British Propaganda in Ireland 1920* by Brian P. Murphy.

77   *Irish Times*, 1 December 1920.

78   The *Times*, 2 December 1920.

79   Seán O'Hegarty, OC Cork No. 1 Brigade to Adjutant-General O'Sullivan, 17 November 1921, A/0535, MA.

80   *Cork Examiner*, 1 December, 1920.

81   *Ibid.*, 25 November 1920.

82   *Ibid.*

83   *Freemans' Journal*, 30 November 1920.

84   *Cork Examiner*, 1 December 1920.

85   O'Donoghue, Florence (ed.), *Rebel Cork's Fighting Story* (Anvil Books, Tralee, 1961), p. 120.

86   *Cork Examiner*, 7 December 1920.

87   Quoted in Abbott, *Police Casualties in Ireland*, p. 178.

88   Report of the British Labour Commission to Ireland (London 1921).

89   *Ibid.*

90   *Who Burnt Cork City?* p. 21.

91   Anna Horgan to Richard Mulcahy, minister of defence, 28 August 1922, A/0535, MA.

92   Intelligence officer McCarthy to Major-General Emmet Dalton, OC Southern Area, 6 September 1922. Report forwarded to minister of defence, Richard Mulcahy, by Dalton, A/0535, MA.

93   Information contained in letter from Comdt Jack McCarthy to Major-General Emmet Dalton, OC, Southern Area, 6 September 1922.

94   *Cork Examiner*, 10 December 1920.

95   *Cork Examiner*, 11 December 1920.

96   *Irish Times*, 11 December 1920

97   Before the introduction of Martial Law, a person who was found guilty by a court-martial had recourse to the normal legal appeal system. However if one was brought to trial before a military court an appeal could only

be made to the military governor. The man designated military governor for the Munster District was Brigadier General Higginson, the officer commanding the 17th Infantry Brigade.

98   Healy, Seán, WS No 686, BMH.

99   Michael Kenny's War of Independence Pension application provided by Dick Kenny.

100   *Cork Examiner*, 4 March 1921.

101   *The Burning of Cork 1920* – RTÉ Radio documentary transmitted on 18 April 1960

102   Healy, Seán, WS No 686, BMH.

103   Michael Kenny's account of the Dillon's Cross ambush and aftermath as related to his son Dick Kenny

104   *Cork Examiner*, Monday 13 December1920. The paper also gave the following information: Cadet S. K. Chapman of 490 London Road, Westcliff-on-Sea, late of 4th Battalion, London Regiment -died of wounds. Cadets M. C. Barrington, J. L. Emanual, B. C. McMonagle, C. M. Bautley, E. C. Cumming, W. Longhurst, A. Anderton, W. M. Moone, C. Wells and F. H. Miles – wounded; Cadet C. A. Worral – slightly wounded.

105   *Who Burnt Cork?* p. 22–23.

106   Report of the British Labour Commission to Ireland.

107   *The Burning of Cork 1920* – RTÉ Radio documentary

108   *Who Burnt Cork?* p. 26–28.

109   *Ibid.*, p. 29.

110   *Ibid.*, p. 28.

111   *Ibid.*, pp. 38–39.

112   American Commission – Interim Report, p. 84.

113   Neeson, Geraldine, *In My Mind's Eye – The Cork I Knnew and Loved* (Prestige Books, Dublin 2001), p. 93.

114   *The Burning of Cork 1920* – RTÉ Radio documentary

115   *The Burning of Cork: An eyewitness account by Alan J. Ellis* (The Aubane Historical Society, Millstreet Co. Cork, 2004)

116   This account was compiled from evidence given by Patrick Barry and other employees of the Munster Arcade at a compensation claim hearing heard before the Recorder of Cork on 17 February 1921, a report of which appeared in the *Cork Examiner* on the following day.

117   *Who Burnt Cork?* p. 61.

118   *Ibid.*, p. 31.

119   *The Burning of Cork 1920* – RTÉ Radio documentary

120   *Who Burnt Cork?* p. 35.

121   *Ibid.*

122   *Ibid.*

123 *Ibid.*, p. 45.

124 *The Burning of Cork: An Eyewitness Account*, p. 8.

125 *Who Burnt Cork City?* p. 39.

126 *Ibid.*, p. 41.

127 *Ibid.*, pp. 23–24. We have identified this witness as Ellen Coughlan.

128 *The Burning of Cork: An Eyewitness Account*, pp. 8–9.

129 *Who Burnt Cork?* p. 65.

130 *Ibid.*, p. 67.

131 From an account of the night's events related by Michael Kenny to his son Dick, and evidence given by Seán Healy in his witness statement to the Bureau of Military History.

132 William Ellis was born in 1873 and had been elected to Cork Corporation in 1916 as an independent nationalist – he subsequently became acting lord mayor in August1922 when Dónal O'Callahan went 'on the run' following the capture of Cork by a National Army force under the command of General Emmet Dalton.

133 *The Burning of Cork: An Eyewitness Account*, p. 9.

134 *Ibid.*, p. 7.

135 *Who Burnt Cork?* p. 63.

136 *Ibid.*

137 *The Burning of Cork 1920* – RTÉ Radio documentary

138 *Ibid.*

139 *Ibid.*

140 *The Burning of Cork: An Eyewitness Account*, p. 9.

141 *Rebel Cork's Fighting Story*, p. 125.

142 Strickland Diaries, Imperial War Museum

143 *Cork Examiner*, 13 December 1920.

144 *Ibid.*

145 *Ibid.*

146 At this time Alan Ellis was also reporting for the *Irish Bulletin* a newsletter which gave the republican version of events unfolding in Ireland. On 15 December 1920 he was sent to Dublin by Florrie O'Donoghue in order provide a first hand account of the burning of Cork to the editor of the *Bulletin*, Frank Gallagher. However, he was arrested on his way back to Cork some days later and incarcerated in Ship Street Barracks near Dublin Castle.

147 *Cork Examiner*, 14 December 1920

148 *Ibid.*

149 *Ibid.*

150 *Ibid.*

151 *Ibid.*

152 *Ibid.*

153 *Ibid.*

154 *Ibid*

155 *Ibid.*

156 *Ibid.*

157 *Ibid.*

158 *Ibid.*

159 *Ibid.*

160 *Ibid.*

161 *Ibid.*

162 *Ibid.*

163 *Ibid.,* 15 December 1920

164 *Ibid.*

165 *Ibid.*

166 *Ibid.*

167 *Ibid.*

168 *Ibid.*

169 *Ibid.*

170 *Ibid.*

171 *Ibid.*

172 *Ibid.*

173 *Ibid.*

174 *Ibid.*

175 Poland, *Fire Call!* p. 36.

176 *Ibid.*

177 *Cork Examiner,* 13 December 1920. In the immediate aftermath of the burning of Cork many republicans were shaken by the action taken by Bishop Cohalan in threatening to excommunicate members of the Volunteer forces who committed acts of 'murder'. While Cohalan earned the undying enmity of many republicans for this action, it should be examined in its own context. First and foremost, Daniel Cohalan was the Roman Catholic bishop of the dioceses of Cork and in that respect he was responsible for the spiritual welfare of his people. As far as he was concerned, any killing then being undertaken by the Volunteers was 'murder' and was in contravention of the sixth commandment. Therefore as bishop he felt he was morally obliged, and had no other option, than to take every action possible to stop individuals committing crimes that would harm others – and which would place their own souls in jeopardy.

178 *Cork Examiner,* 15 December 1920.

179 *Ibid.*

180 *Ibid.*

181 The *Times*, 14 December 1920.

182 Original Document in Cork Pubic Museum.

183 Fr Donal O'Donovan, *The Murder of Canon Magner and Tadhg Crowley* (Dunmanway, 2005), pp. 6, 33.

184 Canon Thomas J. Magner was born on 15 October 1850 in the parish of Ovens and was the son of John and Catherine Murphy-Magner. On completing his primary education in the local national school he attended St Vincent's Seminary in Cork before going to France where he studied for the priesthood at the Irish College in Paris. Following his ordination in 1881, he returned to Cork and was appointed professor in St Finbarr's Seminary until 1885 when he was sent to the parish of Kinsale as a curate. He subsequently served as a curate in the parishes of Bandon and the North Cathedral and on 10 April took up the appointment of parish priest in Dunmanway.

185 Tadhg Crowley is recorded as being a member of Cork No. 3 Brigade in both *Rebel Cork's Fighting Story* and Tom Barry's *Guerrilla Days in Ireland*.

186 *Cork Examiner*, 16 December 1920.

187 *Ibid.*, 20 December 1920.

188 *Ibid.*, 18 December 1920.

189 *Ibid.*

190 *Ibid.*, 17 December 1920.

191 *Ibid.*

192 *Ibid.*, 16 December 1920.

193 *Who Burnt Cork?* p. 11.

194 *Cork Examiner*, 17 December 1920.

195 *Ibid.*

196 *Ibid.*

197 *Ibid.*

198 *Ibid.*

199 *Ibid.*, 18 December 1920.

200 *Ibid.*, 20 December 1920.

201 *Ibid.*

202 *Ibid.*

203 *Ibid.*

204 Of the five RIC men wounded in this attack two died subsequently; Constable Arthur Thorpe died on 30 December and Constable Ernest Dray died the following day.

205 Notice B 21 January 1921 – authors' collection.

206 *Cork Examiner*, 5 Januray 1921.

207 These instructions were later printed as a small booklet entitled *17th Infantry Brigade – Summary of Important Instructions* and were subse-

quently used by British forces engaged in counter-insurgency operations in other parts of the empire. The full set of instructions can be found in the Strickland papers in the Imperial War Museum.

208   *Cork Examiner*, 17 December 1920.

209   Macready, Gen. Sir C. F. N., *Annals of an Active Life*, p. 321.

210   *Ibid.*, p. 322.

211   RIC Inspector General's and County Inspector's Monthly Confidential Reports, NUI Maynooth.

212   *Ibid.*

213   *Ibid.*

214   *Ibid.*

215   General F. P. Crozier, *Ireland For Ever*, p. 178.

216   *Ibid.*

217   *Ibid.*, pp. 177–178.

218   Copy provided to us by Dick Kenny.

219   *Ibid.*

220   *Cork Examiner*, 16 February 1921.

221   Bishop Cohalan made public the fact that the secret RIC meeting was held in his pastoral letter, issued on Sunday, 19 December 1920.

222   Abbott, *Police Casualties in Ireland*. p. 177.

223   *Rebel Cork's Fighting Story*, p. 120.

Bibliography

Published Works

Abbott, Richard, *Police Casualties in Ireland 1919–1922* (Mercier Press, Cork, 2000).

Barry, Tom, *Guerrilla Days in Ireland* (Mercier Press, Cork, 1955).

— The Reality of the Anglo-Irish War1920–21 in West Cork - Refutations, Corrections and Comments on Liam Deasy's Towards Ireland Free (Tralee n.d.)

Bell, J. Bowyer, *The Secret Army* (Academy Press, Dublin, 1997).

Bennett, Richard, *The Black and Tans* (Barnes and Nobel, New York, 1995).

Borgonovo, John (ed.), *Florence and Josephine O'Donoghue's War of Independence – A Destiny that Shapes our Ends* (Irish Academic Press, Dublin, 2006).

Brown, Charles, *The History of the 7th* (privately published, n.d.).

Callwell, C. E., *Field-Marshal Sir Henry Wilson: His Life and Diaries* (Cassell, London, 1927).

Chavasse, Moirin, *Terence MacSwiney* (Clonmore and Reynolds, Dublin, 1961).

Coogan, Tim Pat, *Michael Collins – A Biography* (Hutchinson, London, 1990).

Costello, Francis J., *Enduring the Most, The Life and Death of Terence MacSwiney* (Brandon Books, Dingle, 1995).

— *The Irish Revolution and its Aftermath* (Irish Academic Press, Dublin, 2003).

Crozier, Brig. General F. P., *Ireland For Ever* (Cedric Chivers Ltd, London, 1971).

Deasy, Liam, *Towards Ireland Free, The West Cork Brigade in the War of*

Independence (Royal Carbery Books, Cork, 1992).

Dwyer, T. Ryle, *The Squad – and the intelligence operations of Michael Collins* (Mercier Press, Cork, 2005).

Gaughan, J. Anthony, *The Memoirs of Constable Jeremiah Mee* (Anvil Books, Dublin, 1975).

Griffith, Kenneth and O'Grady, Timothy, *Curious Journey, An Oral History of Ireland's Unfinished Revolution* (Mercier Press, Cork, 1998).

Hamilton, Nigel, *Monty, The Making of a General, 1887–1942* (McGraw Hill Books, New York, 1981).

Hart, Peter, *The I.R.A. and its Enemies, Violence and Community in Cork, 1916–1923* (Oxford University Press, New York, 1998).

— (ed.), *British Intelligence in Ireland, 1920–21, The Final Reports* (Cork University Press, Cork, 2002).

— *The I.R.A. at War, 1916–1923* (Oxford University Press, Oxford, 2003).

Harvey, Dan and White, Gerry, *The Barracks – A History of Victoria/Collins Barracks, Cork* (Mercier Press, Cork, 1997).

Herlihy, Jim, *The Royal Irish Constabulary – A Complete Alphabetical List of Officers and Men, 1816–1922* (Four Courts Press, Dublin, 1999).

— *The Royal Constabulary – A Short History and Genealogical Guide with a Select List of Medals and Casualties* (Four Courts Press, Dublin, 2000).

— *Royal Irish Constabulary Officers – A Biographical and Genealogical Guide, 1816–1922* (Four Courts Press, Dublin, 2004).

Hopkinson, Michael, *The Irish War of Independence* (Gill and Macmillan, Dublin, 2002).

Kee, Robert, *Ireland, a History* (Weidenfeld and Nicholson, London, 1981).

Kenneally, Ian, 'Reports from a "Bleeding Ireland," *The* Cork Examiner *During the Irish War of Independence*', Journal of the Cork Historical and Archaeological Society, Vol. 108, June 2003.

Lee, Joseph, *Ireland 1912–1985: Politics and Society* (Cambridge University Press, Cambridge, 1989).

MacEoin, UinSeánn, *Survivors* (Argenta Publications, Dublin, 1980).

Macready, Gen. Sir C. F. N., *Annals of an Active Life* (Hutchinson, London, 1924).

Moody, T. W. and Martin, F. X., *The Course of Irish History* (Mercier Press, Cork, 1994).

Moylan, Seán, *Seán Moylan: In His Own Words* (Aubane Historical Society, Cork, 2004)

Mulcahy, Gen. Richard, 'Chief of Staff 1919', *Capuchin Annual, 1969.*

Murphy, Brian P., *The Origins & Organisation of British Propaganda in Ireland 1920* (Aubane Historical Society & Spinwatch, Cork, 2006).

Neeson, Geraldine, *In My Mind's Eye – The Cork I Knew and Loved* (Prestige Books, Dublin, 2001).

O'Donoghue, Florence, *Tomás MacCurtain, Soldier and Patriot* (Anvil Books, Tralee, 1955).

— (ed.), *Rebel Cork's Fighting Story* (Anvil Books, Tralee, 1961).

— 'Guerrilla Warfare in Ireland', *An Cosantóir*, Vol. XX, May 1963.

— 'The Reorganisation of the Irish Volunteers', *Capuchin Annual*, 1967.

— *No Other Law* (Anvil Books, Dublin, 1986).

O'Hegarty, P. S., *The Victory of Sinn Féin* (Talbot Press, Dublin, 1924).

O'Kelly, Donal, 'Ordeal By Fire – How the City Faced the Terror of 1920 and 1921', *Rebel Cork's Fighting Story* (Anvil Books, Tralee, 1961).

O'Malley, Ernie, *On Another Man's Wound* (Anvil Books, Dublin, 1979).

Ó Súilleabháin, Michael, *Where the Mountainy Men Have Sown* (Anvil Books, Dublin, 1965).

Poland, Patrick, *'Firecall'! – Cork Fire Brigade Centenary Review 1877–1977* (The Society of St Florian, Cork, 1977).

Russell, Liam, 'Some Activities in Cork City 1920–21', *Capuchin Annual, 1970.*

Ryan, Meda, *Tom Barry, IRA Freedom Fighter* (Mercier Press, Cork, 2003).

Sheehan, William, *British Voices From the Irish War of Independence 1918–1921* (The Collins Press, Cork, 2005).

Townsend, Charles, *The British Campaign in Ireland 1919–1921: The Development of Political and Military Policies* (Oxford University Press, London, 1975).

Valiulis, Maryann Gialanella, *General Richard Mulcahy* (Irish Academic Press, Dublin, 1992).

White, Gerry and O'Shea, Brendan, *The Irish Volunteer Soldier 1913–1923* (Osprey Press, Oxford, 2003).

— *Baptised in Blood – The Formation of the Cork Brigade of Irish Volunteers 1913–1916* (Mercier Press, Cork, 2005).

— 'The Night That Cork Burned', *Cork Holly Bough*, 2005.

Whyte, Louis, *The Wild Heather Glen – The Kilmichael Story of Grief and Glory* (The Kilmichael/Crossbarry Commemoration Committee, Cork, 1995).

Newspapers and Periodicals

An Cosantóir
An tÓglach
Cork Examiner
Cork Holly Bough
Cork Weekly News
Freeman's Journal
Irish Bulletin
Irish Times
London Times
The Nation
Weekly Summary

Booklets

American Commission on the Conditions in Ireland Interim Report (Hardin & Moore Ltd., London, 1921).

Kilmichael: The False Surrender – A Discussion by Peter Hart, Pádraig Ó Cunachain, D. R. O'Connor Lysaght, Dr. Brian P. Murphy and Meda Ryan (Aubane Historical Society, Cork, 1999).

Report of the British Labour Commission to Ireland (London, 1921).

The Burning of Cork: An eyewitness account by Alan J. Ellis (Aubane Historical Society, Cork, 2004).

Who Burnt Cork City? (Irish Labour and Trade Union Congress, Dublin, 1921).

Journals

An Cosantóir – The Irish Defence Forces Magazine

Primary Sources

Cork

Cork Archives Institute

– Seamus Fitzgerald Papers

– Robert Langford Papers

– Liam de Róiste Diaries

– Tomás MacCurtain Papers

– Terence MacSwiney Papers

– Seán O'Hegarty Papers

NUI Maynooth

– British in Ireland Series (Microfilm)

Dublin

National Library of Ireland

– Florence O'Donoghue Papers

University College Dublin

– Richard Mulcahy Papers

– Ernie O'Malley notebooks: – containing interviews with the following veterans of the War of Independence in Cork: Charlie Brown,

Martin Corry, Tom Crofts, Seán Culhane, Dan 'Sandow' Donovan, Seamus Fitzgerald, Dan Healy, Seán Hendrick, Michael Leahy, Pat Margetts, Mick Murphy, Seamus Murphy, Patrick 'Pa' Murray, Connie Neenan, Florence O'Donoghue.

Irish Military Archives, Cathal Brugha Barracks, Dublin

– Bureau of Military History: statements of Robert Ahern, Seán Culhane, Daniel Healy, Mick Murphy, Patrick Murray

– The Collins Papers: documentation relating to personnel who were abducted and executed by Cork No. 1 Brigade, IRA :'Executions by IRA', 'British Casualties, Military" statement by Captain O'Dwyer

London

Imperial War Museum

– General E. P. Strickland Papers: History of the 6th Division in Ireland

– Strickland Diaries

RTÉ Radio Documentary

The Burning of Cork 1920, transmitted on 18 April 1960

Unpublished Works

Borgonovo, John M., *Informers, Intelligence and the 'Anti-Sinn Féin Society'* – *the Anglo-Irish Conflict in Cork City 1920–1921*, MA Thesis (UCC, Cork, 1997).

Girvin, Kevin Edward, *The Life and Times of Seán O'Hegarty* (1891 to 1963) O/C First Cork Brigade, War of Independence, Mphil Thesis (UCC, Cork, 2003).

INDEX